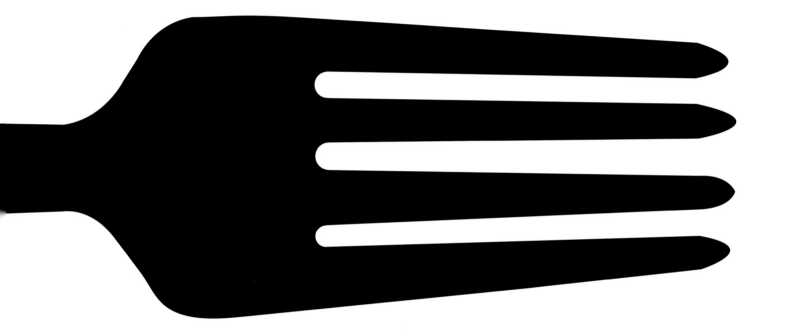

Eat Me.

Classic City Cooking

CELEBRATING THE CHEFS & RESTAURANTS OF ATHENS, GEORGIA

by Juanina Cantrell Kocher

photography by J.P. Bond | foreword by Chef Peter Dale

Alpharetta, Georgia

ISBN: 978-1-61005-697-7
Library of Congress Control Number: 2015921144

10 9 8 7 6 5 4 3 2   0 2 0 9 1 6

Printed in China

Cover Design: Bond Creative Group
Photography: J.P. Bond

♾ This paper meets the requirements of ANSI/NISO Z39.48-1992 (Permanence of Paper)

Contents
&
Introduction

CONTENTS

FOREWORD ix

ACKNOWLEDGMENTS xi

INTRODUCTION. xiii

HOW TO LEARN FROM THIS COOKBOOK xv

5 & 10 3
    PASTA RIBBONS 4
        BASIC TOMATO SAUCE 6
        BASIC PASTA DOUGH. 6
    THE ARNOLD BOMBER 7

THE BRANDED BUTCHER 9
    GOBI AMERICANO. 10
        BBQ SAUCE 10
    SCOTCH EGG 12
        WHISKEY GASTRIQUE | CELERY ROOT REMOULADE. 12

CHOPS & HOPS 14
    ROSEMARY HONEY GLAZE 17
    CURRIED APPLE CHUTNEY 19

DePALMA'S ITALIAN CAFÉ 21
    SEAFOOD CHARMAINE FETTUCCINE 22
        CHARMAINE SAUCE 22
    CRAWFISH PIE BY ANDRÉ DUCOTÉ 24

HEIRLOOM CAFÉ AND FRESH MARKET 26
    CHICKEN MULL 28
        HOUSE-MADE SALTINES 28
    CHILLED SUMMER SQUASH SOUP 30
        PICKLED STRAWBERRIES 30

HOME.MADE. 32
    MARINATED MUSHROOMS 34
    TOASTED PECAN CHICKEN SALAD 36
    CHARRED VIDALIA DIP 36

LAST RESORT GRILL 39
    CRISPY PORK BELLY 40
        PICKLED TOMATILLO. 40
        CACTUS VINAIGRETTE | GREEN RICE 42
    POMPANO 43
        CHARRED JALAPEÑO TARTAR 43
        SHRIMP GRITS | GRAPEFRUIT ROYALS 45

CONTENTS

MAMA'S BOY 47
    VEGETABLE & POTATO HASH 48
    CHEESE GRITS & HOMEMADE BISCUITS 50

THE NATIONAL 52
    LAMB MEATBALLS 54
    CUCUMBER GAZPACHO 56
    THE NATIONAL TONIC 56

THE PINE 59
    HOISIN BRAISED PORK SHOULDER 60
      MISO SOY PICKLES | SWEET CHILI MAYO 60

THE ROYAL PEASANT 62
    SHEPHERD'S PIE 65
    STICKY TOFFEE PUDDING 66
    BANGERS AND MASH 69

SEABEAR OYSTER BAR 71
    SEABEAR CLASSIC CLAM CHOWDER 72
    SHRIMP & CRAB CAKES 74

SPEAKEASY 76
    SUGAR COOKIES 78
      CREAM CHEESE FROSTING 78
    WARM SPINACH DIP 80

VIVA! ARGENTINE CUISINE 82
    TRADITIONAL GROUND BEEF EMPANADAS 84
      HOUSE SEASONING 84
    BUTTERNUT SQUASH BISQUE 86

HONORABLE MENTIONS 89
MAKERS & SHAPERS 97
THE TEAM 109
INDEX 113

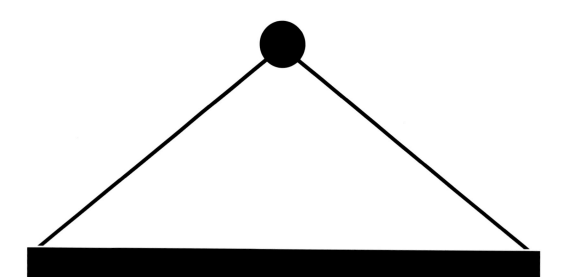

"We have long been known for music and art, and now food, drink, and hospitality are taking center stage as well."

— Chef Peter Dale

I first met Juanina Kocher in 2013 when she had lunch at my restaurant, The National, in Athens, Georgia. She shared with me her dream of writing a cookbook celebrating the restaurants and cuisine of Athens, known to us as the Classic City. I loved her enthusiasm, but truthfully I harbored some skepticism if such an ambitious project could ever come together. Chefs are a notoriously tough crowd to wrangle. Being that she lives in New York, face-to-face meetings were infrequent, which was a shame because her charm and tenacity made it hard to say no to her. With great delight, I can now say I was dead wrong about this project. Despite distance, chefs missing deadlines, and countless hours of work and frustrations, *Classic City Cooking* is now a beautiful book everyone in Athens, and beyond, will treasure for generations.

Classic City Cooking comes to us at a perfect moment in Athens's culinary history. This city has not always been a culinary destination; this is a fairly recent development. Fundamentally, Athens is a college town. The thousands of students who provide Athens with purpose, youth, and vitality have often sought food akin to the lowest common denominator. Fast, cheap, filling, available late night—these have been the qualities most desired by our student population. Our options for cooking at home were limited as well. Experimenting with new flavors or ingredients, not to mention a decent baguette, required an hour-and-a-half (pre-Highway 316) trip to the DeKalb Farmers Market.

Growing up on the East Side of Athens in the '80s, I distinctly remember two exciting events at our neighborhood grocery store. On one occasion, my father, born in New York State, was astounded to find not only the Sunday *New York Times* but also fresh bagels in the bakery. He purchased both right away, along with a package of cream cheese. This would change our Sunday morning routine forever. Not long after, my Ecuadorian mother was delighted to find cilantro next to the curly parsley in the produce department. Today, bagels and cilantro could not be more normal grocery items, but at the time it marked a turning point to me. This sleepy college town was starting to wake up.

We love traditional Southern foods in Athens. I cannot get enough pimento cheese, fried okra, collard greens, and the like. As I write this, the summer heat outside is thick. Fat tomatoes are ripening, and all I can think about are tomato sandwiches on white bread with Duke's Mayonnaise and a little salt and black pepper. Few things could be more perfect.

Athens embraces what is classic and familiar. More importantly, we also welcome what is new and surprising to us. Our college students, with a seemingly basic palate, are also fearless and open to expanding boundaries. Students are discovering the joys of cooking and farming, and many of them choose to stay in Athens long after their studies are over. The town that once lacked bagels and cilantro now boasts expansive farmers markets, multiple breweries, artisanal bakeries, chocolate shops, and more on the way. Athens's larder is full and rich.

Chefs and restaurants embrace Athens's history and sense of place, combining that with innovation and inspiration from afar. This is creating a culinary dialogue unique to Athens, documented by Juanina in *Classic City Cooking*. We have long been known for music and art, and now food, drink, and hospitality are taking center stage as well. Thank you, Juanina Kocher, for making this book happen.

Chef Peter Dale

As the main street through historic Downtown Athens, College Avenue is a bustling street filled with coffee shops, local retailers, and restaurants.

ACKNOWLEDGMENTS

I'd like to thank everyone who believed in this project from the very beginning.

A big thank you to all of my family and friends for their continuous support. Thank you to my parents, James and Yong Cantrell, for always being there, even if from afar.

To my "soul mates," Michelle Callahan, Theresa Napoli, and Malle Quintero, for gifting as many copies of this book as possible.

Thank you to my sister and her husband, Angelina and Jonathon Streetman, for driving me around this great city on my many visits from New York.

To my husband, Ryan Kocher, for all of his support, creative input, and proofreading skills.

J.P. Bond, our amazing photographer, and Brittany Hodges, contributor, for being my partners in crime throughout this crazy process.

This book is a tribute to ALL of our participating chefs and restaurants that continue making Athens one of the best food cities in the South. Thank you to all of the participants and investors for making this book happen.

Special thanks goes to John DeMent, Trish Schneider Cullins, Jordan Snow, Mary Snow, Jerry and Linda Kocher, Barbara Smalley, Wendy Nilsen Pollitzer, Omar and Sarah Mojena, Paul Wagtouicz, J.T. Jensen, Dara Levine, and the team at BookLogix.

Enthusiastically,
Juanina Kocher

Athens's historic Normaltown area has seen a lot of revitalization and is now home to many local eateries and pubs.

INTRODUCTION

Athens is widely reputed as many things: home to the Georgia Bulldawgs, birthplace of musical talents such as REM and the B-52's, the South's "Classic City," and one of America's favorite college towns. This beautiful cultural haven is an ideal setting for up-and-coming artists and businesspeople alike to settle in and expand their professional horizons. Those who yearn for a taste of city life often find this enlightened suburb's proximity to the bustling streets of Atlanta provides the perfect combination of down-home nostalgia and modern urban influence. It is this rare combination that makes Athens so unique. Athenians have the best of everything right outside their door, whilst maintaining the simple ability to enjoy the welcoming, delectable tastes of Southern hospitality. It is, therefore, no surprise to this enthusiastic Southerner that Athens's eclectic menu of spectacular cuisine is now recognized as the true foodie's college town treasure.

The world of food has truly transformed over the past decade. With the help of the Food Network, the Cooking Channel, and multiple social media outlets, restaurants are the new hot spots and chefs have enjoyed an unprecedented level of celebrity. The world of highbrow culinary exclusivity is no longer restricted to large urban centers such as Paris and New York. Therefore, thanks to the bold creativity of a new generation of chefs and restaurateurs, culinary interest has spread like wildfire.

This book was created to showcase Athens as the hip, exciting college town it already is but with an additional focus on food and beverage. Athens is a foodie's paradise, employing an eclectic mix of cuisines, ranging from French to Mexican with everything in between. There is an abundance of cheap eats, specialty bakeries, and, recently, renowned celebrity chefs. In addition to showcasing the already celebrated culinary destinations, I would also like to focus on the "hidden gems" that, until now, only the locals have come to recognize. Athens is more than just a pleasant college town; it is a blossoming landscape of new ideas, cultures, and innovations that are truly reminiscent of its namesake, complete with an electrifying live music scene, an abundance of local artists, and a creative populace that is eager to make its mark on society. This up-and-coming culinary Eden has officially arrived and certainly earned its nickname, the "Classic City."

> *" Athens is more than just a pleasant college town; it is a blossoming landscape of new ideas, cultures, and innovations ... "*

Local shops like The Healthy Gourmet offer a plethora of
unique and taste-enhancing salts, spices, chocolates, wines, and more.

HOW TO LEARN FROM THIS COOKBOOK

I t is important to note that many factors affected which restaurants were chosen to appear in this book. It was not my intention to purposefully exclude any of my hometown's culinary favorites. However, reasons such as page count, recipe releases, and deadlines were all taken into account upon finalization of this project. I would like everyone to know that the Classic City is chock-full of other established staples and newly blossoming hidden gems waiting to be discovered. It is my hope that you will now get out there and taste all that Athens, Georgia, has to offer!

All of the recipes in this book have been tailored for the home chef. That being said, the recipes range from simple, with only a few ingredients, to advanced, with incredibly detailed instructions and a legit grocery list. Cooking is about the love of food and the process of creating a beautiful meal. It should never feel like a chore. If you come across a recipe you want to try but it seems overwhelming or you're short on time, feel free to make adjustments. Make these recipes your own. If the mere thought of creating a sauce or dressing from scratch sends you into a panic, use store-bought ingredients and enjoy the rest of the process. No judgments. Entertaining, cooking, and, of course, eating should always be a pleasurable experience. A few tips: use organic, locally-sourced, and in-season ingredients as much as possible. It will really make a difference in the final product. Smile through the tough stuff. Cooking is a learning experience. Not everyone is a master chef their first—or second, third, fourth—time in the kitchen. If a recipe doesn't come out to your liking, make a few adjustments and try again. Practice makes perfect. Season well (very well) and taste often. Whether you're cooking for yourself on a quiet night in or having a dinner party with a group of loved ones, be thankful for the experience and good fortune you have in being able to create and enjoy a good meal.

Now let's get cookin'!

RESTAURANTS

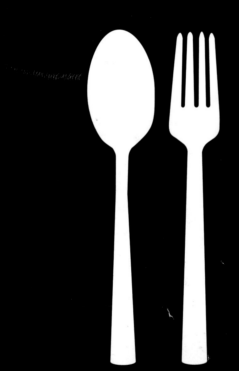

1073 S. MILLEDGE AVENUE
ATHENS, GA 30605
(706) 546-7300

www.fiveandten.com

HUGH ACHESON • CHEF AND OWNER

"The menu," says Hugh, "is an open interpretation of Southern food, melding Georgia cookery with French and Italian influences I learned growing up. It's been a very fun, dynamic restaurant over the years." Acheson's fresh approach to Southern food has earned him a great deal of recognition, including *Food & Wine's* Best New Chef (2002), *The Atlanta Journal-Constitution* Restaurant of the Year (2007), a six-time (2007, 2008, 2009, 2010, 2011, 2012) James Beard nominee, and 2012 winner for Best Chef Southeast. Hugh has also been featured in *Bon Appetit, The New York Times, Food & Wine, Gourmet, Southern Living, Better Homes & Gardens, SAVEUR, Top Chef,* and *Top Chef Masters.*

Hugh was born and raised in Ottawa, Canada, and began working in restaurants at the age of fifteen. Over the years, Hugh has developed a scintillating style of his own, successfully fusing the rich beauty of the American South with the delicate flavors of European cuisine. In March of 2000, he opened his critically-acclaimed flagship restaurant, 5 & 10. Even though Hugh's resume is quite impressive and his culinary star continues to rise, many local Athenians still know him as the unassuming restaurant owner—with a trademarked unibrow—whose restaurants continue to dazzle with beautiful, tasty expressions of his culinary genius.

PASTA RIBBONS
WITH JALAPEÑOS, MOZZARELLA, TOMATOES & PARMESAN

Serves 4

- 1/4 cup kosher salt
- 1 tablespoon olive oil
- 1/4 cup red onion, thinly sliced
- 1/8 cup jalapeños, thinly sliced
- 2 cups tomato sauce (recipe included)
- Basic Pasta Dough (recipe included)
- 3 slices fresh mozzarella, quartered
- 1 cup Parmigiano-Reggiano
- 8 leaves basil (optional)
- Chili flakes (optional)

Fill a large pot with water and add about 1/4 cup of salt. Bring to a boil and reserve for cooking the pasta. In a medium sauté pan, warm the olive oil over medium heat.

Add red onions and sweat briefly. Once the onions are translucent, add the jalapeños and cook for 2 more minutes. Add the tomato sauce and reduce the heat to a simmer. While the sauce is simmering, add the pasta to the boiling water. (Please note: fresh pasta cooks very quickly, taking 1 to 2 minutes at most.) Once your pasta is cooked, drain and reserve about 1 cup of the pasta water.

Add the noodles to the tomato sauce and use reserved pasta water to thin your sauce as needed. Add mozzarella slices and Parmigiano-Reggiano. Toss well. Garnish with a few basil leaves and some chili flakes if desired.

BASIC TOMATO SAUCE

- · 1 cup extra virgin olive oil
- · 4 yellow onions, finely diced
- · 2 carrots, shredded
- · 2 heads garlic, peeled and minced
- · 1 cup tomato paste
- · 2 cans tomatoes, lightly pureed (a stick blender works well!)
- · Bouquet of parsley, thyme, rosemary, and bay leaves
- · Kosher salt

Heat olive oil in large rondeau pot over low heat. Add the onions, carrots, and garlic. Cook until soft, about 20 minutes. Add the tomato paste and stir to coat the vegetables. Add the tomatoes and bouquet. Bring the heat up to a simmer and cook for 45 minutes, stirring occasionally to prevent sticking. Salt to your liking.

BASIC PASTA DOUGH

- · 1 cup flour
- · 1 egg
- · 1 tablespoon olive oil
- · 1 tablespoon water

Put the flour in a mixing bowl and make a well in the center. Mix the water, egg, and olive oil together and pour the mixture into the center of the well. Using a small whisk, gradually incorporate the mixture with the flour until completely combined and it begins to form a ball. Remove from the mixing bowl and begin kneading the dough until it begins to lightly spring back. Wrap in plastic wrap and let sit for 30 minutes. After letting the dough rest, roll the dough through a pasta machine in your shape of choice.

THE ARNOLD BOMBER

This cocktail is the epitome of what the South is all about. It's simple, clean, and a twist on a Southern classic.*

- · 1 liter good-quality gin
- · 1/2 cup loose Earl Grey tea
- · 1/4 cup honey
- · 3 lemons
- · Ice cubes
- · 1 cup homemade lemonade (store-bought works as well)

Using a microplane, zest 2 of the lemons. Whisk the zest, gin, tea, and honey together and let the mixture sit for 1 to 2 hours until the gin takes on the color of iced tea. Strain the liquid through a fine strainer and then through a coffee filter. Store the strained liquid in the gin bottle of the gin used. Fill a collins glass with ice cubes and measure in 2 ounces of the Earl Grey gin. Fill the remainder of the glass with lemonade. Turn the contents of the glass into a cocktail shaker and lightly shake. Return the contents to the glass and garnish with lemon slices.

*What Is An Arnold Palmer?

An Arnold Palmer is traditionally a non-alcoholic beverage consisting of iced tea and lemonade, named after American golfer Arnold Palmer. As the story goes, Palmer ordered the drink at the bar at the Cherry Hills Country Club during the US Open in 1960. A woman overheard him and ordered the drink using the golfer's name and it has been named after him ever since. Well ... now we know!

THE BRANDED BUTCHER

225 N. Lumpkin Street
Athens, Georgia 30601
(706) 850-5152

www.thebrandedbutcher.com

TREY RAYBURN • EXECUTIVE CHEF

*F*ocusing on locally sourced, organic produce, pasture-raised meats, and an elevated appreciation for the elusive arts of charcuterie and oyster shucking, The Branded Butcher has become an essential favorite to Athenians. This popular spot has garnered compliments and praise from a myriad of media outlets, including but not limited to *Zagat*, *Saveur*, and *The New York Times*. Their brunch is a particular crowd pleaser, serving up deliciously witty combinations such as "The Hipster Breakfast," which includes a 16-ounce Pabst Blue Ribbon as a boozy bonus.

Chef Trey Rayburn was destined for a career in the culinary arts. When he was just fifteen years old, he was already working alongside James Beard Award-winning Chef Frank Stitt in Rayburn's hometown of Birmingham, Alabama. After college, Trey went on to study at the French Culinary Institute. He then moved to the Classic City and began working under Chef Matt Palmerlee at Farm 255. The duo made their way over to The Branded Butcher, and after Matt's recent move to Atlanta, Trey was a shoe-in as The Branded Butcher's new executive chef. Although Trey's culinary background is deeply rooted in Southern cuisine, he has very successfully fused his love for bold Latin and Asian flavors with contemporary American fare. Chef Rayburn's dynamic and innovative dishes are as distinctive as the man himself.

GOBI AMERICANO

Serves 2 to 4

- 1/2 cup rice flour
- 1/2 cup cornstarch
- 2/3 cup soda water
- 1 teaspoon baking soda
- 1 teaspoon baking powder
- 2 ounces BBQ Sauce (recipe included)
- 5 ounces cauliflower florets
- 1/4 ounce mustard oil
- Fresh cilantro to garnish

To make the tempura, combine rice flour, cornstarch, 1 teaspoon salt, baking soda, and baking powder. Mix dry ingredients and then slowly add in the soda water. Best to mix by hand so it's not overworked. In a medium bowl, mix the cauliflower and tempura until the cauliflower is completely coated. Carefully drop cauliflower into 350°F frying oil. If using a pot to deep fry, about 1-inch depth is recommended. Serve with BBQ sauce and top with cilantro to garnish.

BBQ SAUCE

- 1/2 medium onion, diced
- 2 fresh jalapeños, diced
- 1/4 cup brown sugar
- 2 cloves garlic
- 1 cup soy sauce
- 1 medium orange, zest and juice
- 1/4 cup sherry vinegar
- 1/4 cup balsamic vinegar
- 1/4 cup ketchup
- 3 teaspoons Worcestershire sauce

Start by sweating the onions and jalapeños in a medium-sized pot. Add in the rest of the ingredients and simmer for 15 minutes. Remove from heat and let cook slightly. Blend in a food processor or blender until smooth.

SCOTCH EGG

Serves 1 to 2

- 1 large egg
- 3 ounces breakfast sausage of choice
- 1/4 cup flour
- 1/4 cup panko bread crumbs
- 1 egg for egg wash
- 2 ounces Celery Root Remoulade (recipe included)
- 3/4 ounce Whiskey Gastrique (recipe included)
- 1/4 cup iodized salt
- 1 pushpin
  Chef's note: We like to put a pushpin in the bottom of the egg while boiling because it makes them easier to peel.

Fill a medium-sized pot halfway full with water and add 1/4 cup of iodized salt. Bring to a rolling boil. Drop the egg in the water for exactly 5 minutes and 30 seconds. Remove from the water and place in an ice bath. When completely cooled off, peel the egg and set aside. Wrap the egg completely in a thin layer of breakfast sausage. It spreads out easier by putting it in between two layers of plastic wrap and pressing it out with a rolling pin. Bread the egg and sausage with flour, then egg wash, then bread crumbs. It's now ready to fry or bake. They are fried at the restaurant at 350°F for 3 minutes. To bake, place the egg on a sheet tray at 400°F for 4 minutes. Serve with Whiskey Gastrique and Celery Root Remoulade.

WHISKEY GASTRIQUE

- 1/4 cup apple cider
- 1/4 cup brown sugar
- 1/2 cup sherry vinegar
- 2 teaspoons bourbon
- 1 teaspoon molasses

Combine all of these ingredients, except the bourbon, in a small pot and reduce on medium heat until you have the consistency of syrup. Remove from the heat and stir in the bourbon to finish.

CELERY ROOT REMOULADE

- 1 6-ounce bulb celery root, grated
- 2 teaspoons Duke's Mayonnaise
- 1 teaspoon Dijon mustard
- Juice of 1/2 a lemon
- Pinch salt

Combine all of these ingredients in a mixing bowl and stir until celery root is coated well.

CHOPS & HOPS

2 S. Main Street #112
Watkinsville, GA 30677
(706) 310-1101

www.chopsandhops.com

ANDREW WALLACE, JESSICA WALLACE, PATRICK LANG
& MYCHELL LANG • OWNERS
MATT KOVITCH • CHEF

On 2 South Main Street in Watkinsville, Georgia, you'll find Chops & Hops, a place both familiar and unlike anywhere else. Although a touch outside of Athens proper, the food and friendly ambiance draws in hungry guests from all surrounding counties.

Executive Chef Matt Kovitch uses only the freshest ingredients prepared to order and has a passion for the culinary arts that is unmatched. His drive to constantly fine tune his craft is evident in every plate that leaves his kitchen. An Atlanta native, Matt Kovitch worked his way up from cooking on the line to being the sous chef at Bouchon Bistro, a farm-to-table French comfort food restaurant in Asheville, North Carolina. Chef Kovitch has brilliantly blended his French-inspired techniques with his deep-rooted love for Southern comfort food. He brings his many guests at Chops & Hops a fresh yet classic food menu that pairs perfectly with one of the restaurant's fine wines or plentiful craft beer options.

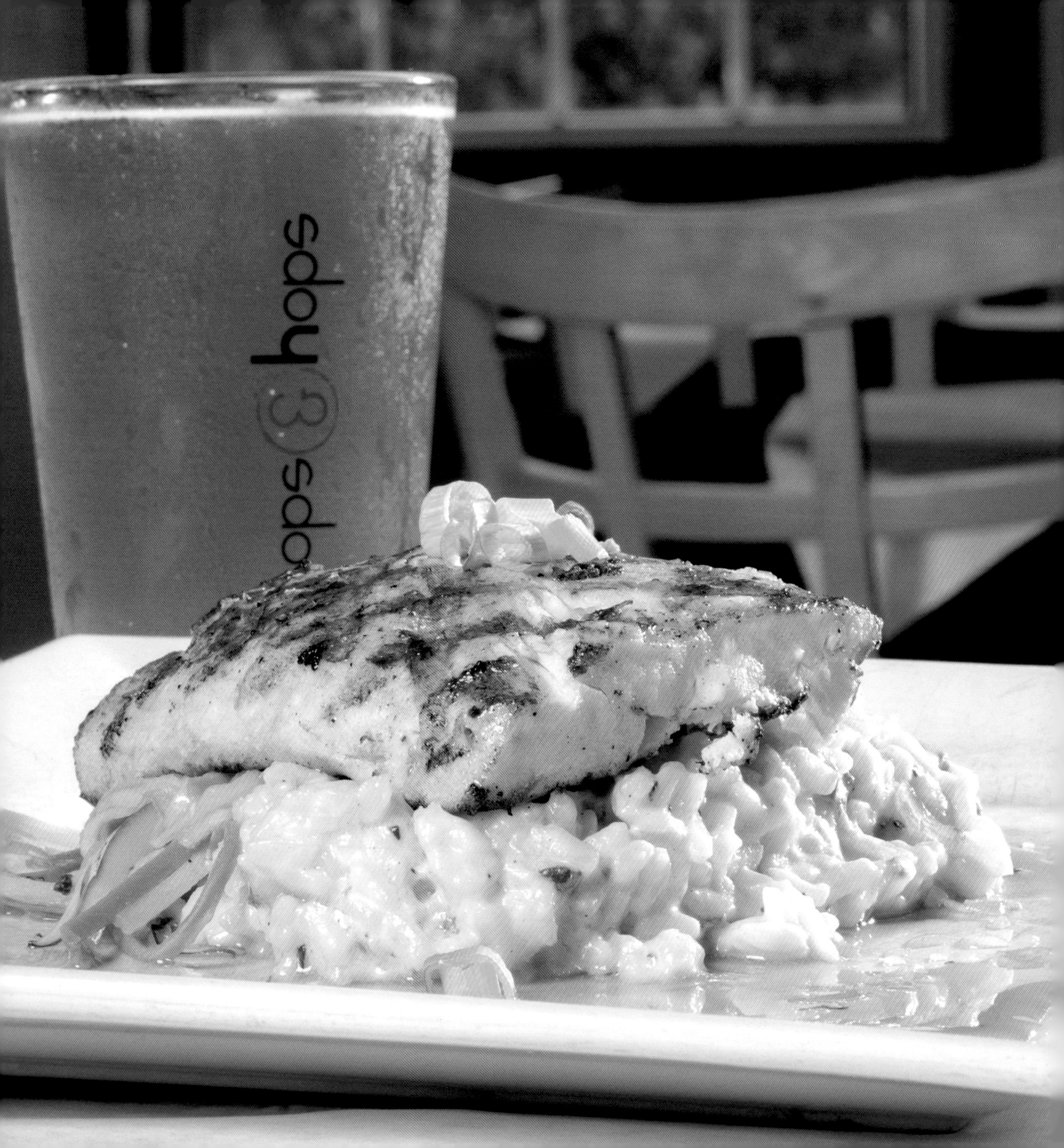
hops

ROSEMARY HONEY GLAZE

Yields about 3 cups

- · 1 tablespoon olive oil
- · 1 small yellow onion, diced
- · 1/2 tablespoon garlic, minced
- · 1 tablespoon white wine
- · 2-1/2 cups honey
- · 1 cup water
- · 2 teaspoons fresh rosemary, finely chopped
- · Kosher salt & pepper

Place oil, onion, and garlic in small stockpot and sauté on medium-high heat until onions are translucent (about 2 minutes). Deglaze the pan with white wine.

Add honey and water. Continue to cook on medium heat for approximately 3 minutes.

Remove from heat and whisk in rosemary, salt, and pepper until fully incorporated.

Chef's note: Perfect with fried calamari or grilled mahi-mahi.

CURRIED APPLE CHUTNEY

Yields about 2 cups

- 3 medium-sized Granny Smith apples, diced
- 1 cup golden raisins
- 1/2 medium-sized yellow onion, finely diced
- 1 cinnamon stick
- 2 star anise
- 2 tablespoons curry powder
- 1/2 cup apple cider vinegar
- 2 bay leaves
- 1/4 cup brown sugar
- 1 tablespoon Dijon mustard
- 2 tablespoons garlic, minced
- 1 tablespoon turmeric
- 1/2 tablespoon cumin
- Kosher salt & pepper, to taste

In small stockpot, combine apples, garlic, and onions. Sauté on medium-high heat until apples slightly caramelize. Add all other ingredients and cook on medium heat until most liquid evaporates, stirring occasionally (approximately 8 minutes).

Let cool in refrigerator for at least 30 minutes. Once cooled, discard star anise, cinnamon stick, and bay leaf and serve!

Chef's note: Excellent on roasted lamb or grilled pork chops. The chutney is also a lovely addition to a cheese plate.

DePALMA'S ITALIAN CAFÉ

East Side Location
1965 Barnett Shoals Road
Athens, GA 30605
Other Locations: Downtown Athens / Timothy Road, Athens
(706) 369-0085

www.depalmasitaliancafe.com

DAVE CAPPI • OWNER
PATRICK MCMASTER, DAVID BROCKWAY & JOHN DUFUR • MANAGING PARTNERS
ANDRÉ DUCOTÉ • EAST SIDE CHEF

DePalma's East Side opened on May 11, 1992, and has been going strong ever since. This was the second DePalma's location in town, following the format of the original located in the heart of Downtown Athens. This cozy spot can be found on 1965 Barnett Shoals Road in the Green Acres Shopping Center. The atmosphere on the East Side is laid back and comfortable. Think big comfy booths, colorful stained glass, recycled old growth maple floors, and artsy decor. All of these components make DePalma's an easygoing yet warm place to dine out in Athens. The collection of customer-signed wine bottles includes many weddings, anniversaries, and first date memories that the team at DePalma's have grown to cherish.

Although born in *Lafayette, Louisiana,* André Ducoté was primarily raised in Metro Atlanta. He moved to Athens in 2006 to take advantage of the legendary music scene. Since 2009, he has found a love and passion for cooking that has been fostered by his five-plus years at the East Side DePalma's. André has generously shared two of his best recipes. The first is an adaptation from a sauce that has been cooked up at DePalma's for over twenty years. The second is a side he regularly pairs with his fresh catch on Thursday nights.

SEAFOOD CHARMAINE FETTUCCINE

Serves 8 to 10

- · Cold Charmaine Sauce with spinach and basil (recipe included)
- · 1 pound large shrimp, cleaned
- · 2-1/2 pounds U10 sea scallops
- · 2 tablespoons clarified butter
- · 2 pounds fresh or dry fettuccine noodles
- · 1 cup Parmesan, grated
- · Italian parsley or basil to garnish

CHARMAINE SAUCE

- · 1/2 cup fresh basil, chopped
- · 1 cup fresh spinach, finely chopped
- · 1 cup vine ripe tomatoes, chopped
- · 1/3 cup sundried tomatoes, chopped
- · 1/2 cup Parmesan, grated
- · 1/4 cup scallions, chopped
- · 1/4 cup jalapeños, chopped
- · 1/4 cup fresh lime juice
- · 1/4 cup fresh garlic, chopped
- · 1/2 cup extra virgin olive oil
- · 1-1/2 teaspoon ancho chili powder
- · 3 anchovy fillets, minced very fine (optional but a nice touch and adds flavor)
- · 1 quart heavy cream

The story that Chef heard when we first got this recipe was that it was a sauce named after a waitress who was being courted by a chef in New Orleans. It was originally tossed with fresh penne. In our version, the sauce is cooked down to meld the flavors. The original recipe appeared in FOOD & WINE over twenty years ago.

– Patrick McMaster, Managing Partner

Heat clarified butter in a large sauté pan. Salt and pepper your seafood to taste. Sauté shrimp and scallops until cooked. Shrimp should just turn pink and scallops firm but tender. Be careful not to overcook. Set aside and cover to keep warm.

Cook your pasta according to package instructions. While your pasta is cooking, combine the first 12 ingredients for the Charmaine Sauce in a large pan. Put half the basil and half the spinach to the side. Sauté over medium heat for about 5 minutes, until the tomatoes and jalapeños are just cooked and the ingredients are well incorporated. Slowly add heavy cream until you've reached a nice, creamy consistency. Remove from heat. Stir in remaining basil and spinach. Salt and pepper to taste. Cook pasta until al dente. It should have a nice bite. DO NOT overcook. Toss with the Charmaine Sauce. Top with shrimp and scallops. Finish off the dish with grated Parmesan and a parsley or basil garnish.

DePalma's Italian Café

CRAWFISH PIE BY ANDRÉ DUCOTÉ

Serves 6 to 8

- 1/2 stick butter
- 1/2 red onion, diced
- 1/2 red bell pepper, diced
- 1/2 green bell pepper, diced
- 1 stick celery, diced
- 1 clove garlic, minced
- 2 fresh ears summer corn, cut from the cob
- 2 uncooked scrambled eggs (reserve for later)
- 1 pound cooked crawfish (reserve for later)

Sauté the first 7 items until tender, then turn heat down and simmer for 10 minutes to create the base. Add the following after the base is ready and combine thoroughly.

- 8 ounces mascarpone cheese
- 1 cup heavy cream
- 1 tablespoon kosher salt
- 1 teaspoon cayenne
- 2 teaspoons smoked paprika
- 2 teaspoons sugar
- 2 teaspoons Tabasco Original Red Sauce

Cook until all cheese has melted and the cream has reduced. Add one pound of cooked crawfish and cool completely in refrigerator. Add 2 uncooked scrambled eggs to mixture and mix thoroughly. Pour mixture into a store-bought (or homemade!) 9-inch pre-baked pie crust and bake at 325°F for 20 minutes.

HEIRLOOM CAFÉ AND FRESH MARKET

815 N. Chase Street
Athens, GA 30601
(706) 354-7901

www.heirloomathens.com

JESSICA ROTHACKER & TRAVIS BURCH • OWNERS
JOEL PENN • CHEF

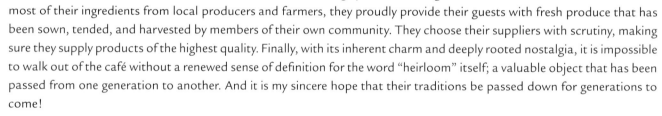

The folks at Heirloom Café and Fresh Market strive passionately to convey a joyous sense of community through their food. The Boulevard neighborhood in Athens is a very special place, full of historic homes of varying styles and people from different backgrounds. The neighborhood is, in and of itself, an heirloom closely protected by the Historic Preservation Committee and its prideful residents.

The food at Heirloom Café and Fresh Market is also something special. Sourcing most of their ingredients from local producers and farmers, they proudly provide their guests with fresh produce that has been sown, tended, and harvested by members of their own community. They choose their suppliers with scrutiny, making sure they supply products of the highest quality. Finally, with its inherent charm and deeply rooted nostalgia, it is impossible to walk out of the café without a renewed sense of definition for the word "heirloom" itself; a valuable object that has been passed from one generation to another. And it is my sincere hope that their traditions be passed down for generations to come!

Chef Joel Penn was born in Manassas, Virginia. His family moved to Georgia when he was a child. In 2003, he relocated to Athens to attend the University of Georgia, where he majored in magazine journalism. Like many students, he fell in love with the Classic City and decided to stick around. He began cooking professionally in 2008. Chef Penn has been cooking up culinary magic in his kitchen ever since.

CHICKEN MULL

Serves 6 to 8

- 1 large roaster or stewing chicken
- 2 cups buttermilk
- 2 large carrots, roughly chopped
- 3 large onions, roughly chopped
- 2 bay leaves
- 4 whole black peppercorns
- Your favorite vinegar-based hot sauce (such as Tabasco Original Red Sauce or Texas Pete Original Hot Sauce), to taste
- Kosher salt, to taste
- House-made Saltines (recipe included)

Add chicken, carrots, onions, bay leaves, and peppercorns to stockpot. Cover with water and simmer on low heat for 8 hours. Remove chicken and let cool. Strain stock and reserve, discarding solids. Shred chicken meat, discarding all bones and skin.

Return stock to medium-high heat and reduce by about 1/3. Add in chicken meat, buttermilk, salt, and hot sauce to taste. Simmer for about 5 minutes to let flavors combine. Finely crumble in some of your homemade saltines to get the stew to your desired thickness. Garnish with saltines and more hot sauce if desired. Serve hot.

Chef's Note: This dish pairs perfectly with a dry white wine or sour beer.

HOUSE-MADE SALTINES

- 4 cups all-purpose flour
- 3/4 cups softened butter
- 1-1/3 cups whole milk
- 1 teaspoon baking powder
- Kosher salt to dust

Mix flour, baking powder, and butter. Add milk. Blend well. Form dough into ball and roll very thin, about 1/8 of an inch thick. Place on an ungreased cookie sheet and prick dough with a fork several times. Dust with salt. Bake at 375°F for 12 to 20 minutes until golden brown. Let cool, then break into shards of any size you like.

CHILLED SUMMER SQUASH SOUP

Serves 6 to 8

- 5 pounds yellow summer squash, washed and roughly chopped
- 2 medium-to-large Vidalia onions, peeled and thinly sliced
- 1-inch piece ginger, peeled and minced
- 4 whole cloves garlic
- 1-1/2 tablespoons madras curry powder
- 1 vanilla bean, split, or 1 teaspoon vanilla extract
- 1 8-ounce can coconut milk

- Vegetable stock, to cover (water is fine if in a pinch)
- Kosher salt, to taste
- 1/2 cup shelled peanuts, toasted and ground to a rough powder in a food processor or mortar & pestle
- Pickled Strawberries (recipe included)
- Fresh basil leaves for garnish
- 2 tablespoons olive oil

Heat about 2 tablespoons of olive oil in a large heavy-bottom stockpot or Dutch oven over medium-high heat. Add onions, garlic, ginger, and curry powder. Sweat vegetables, stirring regularly, for about 4 to 5 minutes. Add squash, vanilla, and coconut milk. Add enough vegetable stock or water to cover the squash. Simmer on medium-low heat for about 20 minutes to soften the squash. Strain out vanilla bean, if used. Allow mixture to cool and blend all contents in a high-speed blender. Strain blended soup through a fine mesh strainer set over a pot or bowl to catch the contents, pressing hard on the solids. Discard solids. Season strained soup with salt to taste. Chill in fridge until cold.

Assemble bowls with peanuts and strawberries on bottom. Ladle soup overtop. Garnish with basil leaves.

Serve with a Spanish rosé or an IPA like Tropicalia

PICKLED STRAWBERRIES

- 1/2 pound ripe summer strawberries, sliced about 1/8 inch thick
- 3 cups distilled white or red wine vinegar (or a mixture of the two)

- 2 cups sugar
- 2 whole star anise
- 2 whole cinnamon sticks
- 2 whole cloves

Combine all but strawberries in a saucepot and bring to a boil over medium-high heat until sugar dissolves. Cool pickle brine completely before pouring over the strawberries.

Put berries in a Mason jar or similar container and pour over the brine, using a saucer or similar item to weigh down the berries under the brine. Pickled strawberries will be ready after one day in the fridge.

HOME.MADE

1072 Baxter Street
Athens, GA 30606
(706) 206-9216

www.homemade-catering.com

MIMI MAUMUS • CHEF / OWNER

Home.made started out as a made-from-scratch catering company specializing in Southern cuisine. Chef Mimi Maumus built home. made slowly over the course of eight years while working as executive sous chef for Hugh Acheson's beloved 5 & 10 restaurant. Home.made is a successful catering company, restaurant, and distributor of signature Southern snacks available nationwide. Chef Maumus's food is modern-yet-classic Southern, a.k.a. "culinary grandma." Her dishes are approachable, creative, thoughtful, and delicious.

Home.made is committed to producing memorable food experiences, using the highest quality ingredients with a skill set that comes from years of conscientious training. Chef Maumus enjoys putting inventive twists on old Southern favorites like pickled deviled eggs, Swanee Bites (cheese straws sandwiched with pimento cheese, rolled in Georgia pecans . . . I mean, genius!), and pepper jelly candied pecans. Fascinated by wild edibles, you can find Southern "weeds" on her menus such as chainey briar (smilax), plantain leaves, wild grapes, and kudzu.

Chef Maumus believes good food begins with good ingredients. Many of the ingredients at home.made are sourced through local farms, including Woodland Gardens, Bartram Trails Farm, Northeast Farmers of Georgia, and Foster Brady.

MARINATED MUSHROOMS

Serves 2 to 4

- · 1-1/2 cups apple cider vinegar
- · 3/4 cup white wine
- · 3 tablespoons kosher salt
- · 1 tablespoon whole coriander seeds, lightly toasted
- · 1 sprig fresh rosemary, 4 to 6 inches long
- · 4 cloves fresh garlic, smashed but not chopped
- · 1/2 pound button mushrooms
- · 1/3 cup olive oil

Combine first 6 ingredients, mix well, and set aside.

In a sauté pan, heat the olive oil until it's just beginning to smoke. Turn off heat and carefully add mushrooms to the pan to sear (watch out for splatters!). Return heat to high. Toss mushrooms until browned on all sides. Turn off heat and add remaining ingredients all at once. Return heat to low for 1 minute. Transfer mushrooms and marinade to a stainless steel or ceramic bowl to cool to room temperature. Refrigerate. Will keep for up to 2 weeks in the refrigerator.

Sweet Fact: The Vidalia onion is a sweet and mild yellow onion grown originally in Toombs County, Georgia. It became the state of Georgia's official state vegetable in 1990.

TOASTED PECAN CHICKEN SALAD

Yields about 1 quart

- 1-1/4 pounds cooked skinless chicken breast (boiled or roasted), diced
- 1 cup mayonnaise
- 1-1/2 teaspoons celery leaves (from the center of a bunch of celery), chopped
- 1-1/2 teaspoons tarragon (fresh or dry); if fresh, then chop
- 1 tablespoon whole grain mustard—home.made uses Zatarain's Creole Mustard
- 1/2 tablespoon lemon zest, grated
- 3 tablespoons toasted pecans, chopped
- 3 tablespoons dried cranberries
- Kosher salt & pepper, to taste

Mix all ingredients except for the chicken thoroughly. Add chicken, season with salt and pepper to taste, and refrigerate. This recipe is delicious alone but wonderful over greens or atop your favorite fresh bread.

CHARRED VIDALIA DIP
Yields about 2 cups

- 2 cups Vidalia onion (if you can't find Vidalia onions, yellow onion will do), diced
- 6 ounces cream cheese, room temperature
- 8 ounces sour cream
- 1 teaspoon onion powder
- 1 teaspoon garlic powder
- 1 teaspoon kosher salt
- Pinch cayenne pepper
- 1 tablespoon parsley
- Juice of 1 lemon

Preheat your oven to 450°F. Roast onions for 5 minutes. Turn oven to broil and cook until onions are blackened on edges but not burned.

Whip all ingredients in a KitchenAid with beater blade or by hand. Serve with your favorite cut vegetables, toast points, or chips.

LAST RESORT GRILL

174-184 W. Clayton Street
Athens, GA 30601
(706) 549-0810

www.lastresortgrill.com

MELISSA CLEGG • CO-OWNER
JAMSHAD "JAMMY" ZARNEGAR • CO-OWNER
AARON PHILLIPS • CHEF

Last Resort's heritage can be traced back to its original designation as a performance venue for up-and-coming musicians in 1966. When Athens began to flourish as a Southern hub for local musical talent, Last Resort's legend had already been born. Its doors had been closed for around a decade when present owner, Melissa Clegg, stepped in to revitalize this piece of Athenian history. In its casual-yet-elevated atmosphere, Last Resort has been serving an assorted fusion of international cuisines to its loyal patrons ever since, with a delicious twist of Southern flavor, of course!

I will always cherish Last Resort as my first "taste of Athens," if you will. To be honest, up until my late teenage years, going out to eat consisted of family nights at Red Lobster and Outback. Nothing against these American classics, but as a senior in high school, after a few friends casually invited me to Last Resort's Sunday brunch, my "foodie" life was forever changed.

Chef Aaron Phillips has been with Last Resort for over eight years. When asked what made him become a chef, he answered, "Honestly, it's not something I sat down and decided. Things I love: food and endless learning opportunities, endless creative opportunities, the fast-paced excitement of service, the slightly dysfunctional family feel of a close restaurant staff (in a good way)." Aaron also credits his mother for his culinary talents. "My mother was incredibly casually talented in a kitchen. She didn't have to even try."

CRISPY PORK BELLY
WITH ROASTED ASPARAGUS & GREEN RICE
Serves 4

- 4 9-ounce portions pork belly
- 2 cups celery, chopped
- 2 cups carrots, peeled and chopped
- 2 cups yellow onion, chopped
- 4 bay leaves
- 4 sprigs rosemary
- 3 sprigs oregano
- 3 sprigs sage
- 5 cups vegetable stock
- 1 pound roasted asparagus
- 2 tablespoons blended oil
- Cactus Vinaigrette (recipe included)
- Pickled Tomatillo (recipe included)
- Green Rice (recipe included)

Preheat oven to 250°F. Season the pork bellies with salt and pepper and let rest for 1/2 hour. Place herbs and vegetables in the bottom of an oven-safe pan with a tight-fitting lid. Layer the bellies on the vegetables and add stock. If the bellies are not submerged, add enough water to cover. With lid on, braise in the oven at 250°F for 3-1/2 to 4 hours. Remove the bellies from the liquid when they can be easily pierced with a fork. Set aside.

Heat 2 tablespoons of blended oil in a sauté pan over high heat. When the oil is almost smoking, add the cooked bellies one at a time with the skin side down. Be careful because the skin will pop. Cook on high until the skin is crisp. Remove and assemble the plate as desired with a green rice base and asparagus and vegetable mixture. Top bellies with desired amount of pickled tomatillo and drizzle plate with cactus vinaigrette. Serve and enjoy!

PICKLED TOMATILLO

- 1 large tomatillo
- 1 cup cane vinegar
- 2 cups water
- 6 tablespoons sugar
- 4 teaspoons salt

Remove husks and wash tomatillo under cold water. Quarter, then half. Combine remaining ingredients in a small saucepan and simmer until sugar and salt have dissolved. Place tomatillos in a container with a tight-fitting lid and pour brine over them to cover. The tomatillo will be ready after about 5 minutes.

CACTUS VINAIGRETTE

- 2 cactus pads (nopales)
- 2 tablespoons cilantro, minced
- 1 tablespoon shallots, minced
- 2 cloves garlic, minced
- 1 teaspoon crushed red pepper

- 1 teaspoon sugar
- 1-1/2 cups neutral oil
- 1/2 cup cane vinegar
- Kosher salt and pepper, to taste

Clean nopales by laying them flat on a cutting board and running a sharp knife against the grain of the needles. Cut off the base and around the edges. Rinse under cold water, making sure all the needles have been removed. Pat dry. Brush with oil and grill, flipping once. They're done when they turn from green to light brown. However, a little bit of char is good. Lightly sauté the shallot and garlic and reserve. Roughly chop the cactus and combine all ingredients, except the oil, in a blender and run until smooth. Add the remaining oil in a light stream. Season to taste.

If you have trouble finding nopales, green bell peppers can be used as a similar substitute.

GREEN RICE

- 1 cup long-grain white rice
- 1 bunch cilantro, chopped
- 1 bunch scallions, thinly sliced
- 2 poblano chili peppers

- 2 cloves garlic
- 2 cups vegetable stock or water
- 1 teaspoon olive oil
- Kosher salt & pepper, to taste

Coat poblanos with the olive oil and place on a sheet pan. Roast poblanos uncovered in 350°F oven for 20 to 30 minutes, turning occasionally. Remove poblanos to a bowl and seal tightly with plastic wrap. Set aside and let cool a bit while steaming. When cool enough to handle, remove the skins, stem, and deseed. Place poblanos, cilantro, and garlic in blender and puree. Adding some of the cooking liquid will help break down this mixture into what should be a paste of sorts. Combine rice, scallions, paste, and remaining cooking liquid in small pot and bring to a boil. Reduce to a simmer and cover. Cook on low without removing the lid for about 20 minutes or until the liquid has been absorbed. Remove from heat, fluff, and season.

POMPANO
WITH SHRIMP GRITS, JALAPEÑO TARTAR, AND GRAPEFRUIT

Serves 4

- 4 pompano fillets, seasoned with salt and pepper
- 2 tablespoons olive or canola oil
- Charred Jalapeno Tartar (recipe included)
- Shrimp Grits (recipe included)
- Grapefruit Royals (recipe included)

Add oil to a sauté pan and sear seasoned fish over medium-high heat, turning once, about 4 minutes per side. Finish in 350°F oven until cooked and flaky. Plate shrimp grits, top with one fillet and Jalapeño Tartar. Garnish with Grapefruit Royals.

CHARRED JALAPEÑO TARTAR

- 2 egg yolks
- 2 cups olive or canola oil
- 2 fresh jalapeños
- 4 teaspoons parsley, minced
- 2 cloves garlic, minced
- 2 teaspoons Dijon mustard
- 2 teaspoons capers, minced
- 1 teaspoon shallots, minced
- 2 tablespoons fresh lemon juice
- Kosher salt & pepper, to taste

Coat the jalapeños using only a couple drops of oil. Skewer the jalapeños and roast over a high flame, turning until the skin is blistered and black and the flesh is just cooked. Cover and set aside to cool. Meanwhile, combine the egg yolks and mustard in a blender and add oil, slowly at first. Continue adding oil until a mayonnaise has formed. Cut the cooled jalapeños in half, remove the seeds, and dice, keeping the charred skin. Combine remaining ingredients in the blender and pulse until combined. Season with salt and pepper to taste.

SHRIMP GRITS

- · 12 medium shrimp, peeled
- · 2 teaspoons Old Bay Seasoning
- · 3/4 cup quick grits
- · 3 cups whole milk
- · 2 teaspoons butter
- · Kosher salt & pepper, to taste

Bring the milk, Old Bay, butter, and shrimp to a simmer in a medium saucepan. When the shrimp are just pink, remove them from the liquid and set aside. Bring the milk to a boil and add the grits while whisking. Remove from heat and continue to whisk until the grits have set. Roughly chop the shrimp and fold into grits. Season with salt and pepper.

GRAPEFRUIT ROYALS

- · 1 large grapefruit

Cut the bottom and top off the grapefruit. Place on cutting board and, using a sharp knife, cut the peel away from the fruit, making sure to remove all of the pith (the white layer under the skin). Over a bowl, remove the segments from the fruit, cutting Vs in between the membrane. The segments should be pure fruit, no pith or membrane.

197 Oak Street
Athens, GA 30601
(706) 548-6249

www.mamasboyathens.com

ALICIA SEGARS & COOPER HUDSON • OWNERS
JEFF DANIELL • CHEF

photo courtesy of Mama's Boy

Mama's Boy Restaurant is a cozy Southern diner offering up delicious takes on breakfast and lunch. Having been consistently voted best breakfast and brunch in Athens by multiple local publications and magazines for the past several years, they've also been featured in *Garden and Gun*, *Southern Living*, *Taste of the South*, and *Cooking with Paula Deen*. They've received well-deserved shout-outs on *Taste of the Town with Todd Blackledge*, *SEC Nation*, and *Southern Fried Road Trip*. Needless to say, the word has spread!

Founders, owners, and best friends Alicia Segars and Cooper Hudson met while working at another Athens favorite and featured restaurant, Last Resort Grill. "We love being a part of the Athens community and celebrating milestones with our awesome customers!" says the dynamic duo. Celebrating almost a decade at their original spot on Oak Street, Mama's Boy is unique to the city. They offer scrumptious breakfast, brunch, and lunch favorites. They also cater! So . . . your place or theirs?

VEGETABLE & POTATO HASH

Serves 2 to 4

- · 2 medium-sized potatoes, washed, boiled to al dente, and diced
- · 5 radishes, halved
- · 5 Brussels sprouts, halved
- · 2 eggs
- · 1/2 cup store-bought or homemade hollandaise sauce
- · 2 tablespoons olive oil
- · 1 teaspoon garlic powder
- · 1 teaspoon blackened seasoning
- · Kosher salt & pepper, to taste

Toss radishes and Brussels sprouts in olive oil, salt, and pepper. Roast vegetables for 8 to 12 minutes, cool, and then quarter. Set aside. Deep or pan-fry diced potatoes in oil and season with blackened seasoning and garlic powder. Add vegetables. To serve, poach both eggs and place atop the vegetable and potato hash. Top with hollandaise sauce and serve immediately.

CHEESE GRITS & HOMEMADE BISCUITS

CHEESE GRITS
Serves 2 to 4

- 1 cup instant grits
- 2 cups water
- 2 cups milk
- 3 tablespoons butter
- 1/4 cup Monterey jack cheese, shredded
- 1/4 cup smoked cheddar, shredded
- Kosher salt & pepper, to taste

Follow package instructions on instant grits. Split the water called for in the instructions with milk (this makes it creamy!). Add cheeses and season to taste.

HOMEMADE BISCUITS
Makes 10 to 12 biscuits

- 3-1/4 cups flour
- 1-1/2 tablespoons baking powder
- 1 tablespoon & 1 teaspoon sugar
- 1/2 teaspoon kosher salt
- 3/4 cups cold butter, diced
- 1-1/4 cups buttermilk

Preheat oven to 350°F. In a large bowl, combine dry ingredients and mix well. Add cold, diced butter and mix in with hands for 2 minutes. Add buttermilk 1/2 a cup at a time, mixing with your hands as you go until the mixture is incorporated. Set dough aside and flour a flat surface. Roll out dough until it's about 3/4 inch thick. Use a round biscuit cutter to cut biscuits. On a sheet pan lined with parchment paper, place biscuits 1/2 inch apart. Bake at 350°F for 10 minutes. Rotate in oven and bake for another 10 minutes until biscuits are golden brown. You can check the middle with a toothpick to be sure. Brush hot biscuits with butter before serving.

Baker's tip: Use a sharp biscuit cutter! The sharp edges will not seal the sides, thus promoting a high-rise result. Glasses and tin cans (while they'll work in a pinch), trap air and compress biscuit dough, sealing the sides and reducing rise.

THE NATIONAL

232 W. Hancock Avenue
Athens, GA 30601
(706) 549-3450

www.thenationalrestaurant.com

PETER DALE • EXECUTIVE CHEF / OWNER

The idea behind The National is simple: to provide a casual neighborhood gathering spot reminiscent of the bars and cafés one enjoys on their travels to Europe and abroad. Mediterranean-inspired food and wine is served for lunch and dinner in the dining room and throughout the day at the bar. While the menu points to culinary traditions from abroad, they value the local farmers and their dishes reflect the changing seasons in Northeast Georgia.

Chef Peter Dale has always loved food and cooking but it wasn't until after college that he started cooking professionally. He worked on Capitol Hill and for the University of Georgia but realized he couldn't bear to sit at a desk all day.

His inspiration? "I find so much inspiration for my food from my travels. I am so fortunate to have grown up in a family that traveled a lot and exposed me to many cultures and cuisines from a young age."

Top Chef Hugh Acheson has been Peter's longtime friend and mentor. The talented duo actually teamed up together to create the idea and concept behind The National. "He [Hugh] is great at letting younger cooks find their own voice rather than repeating what he has already done. Hugh has always been supportive of my interests. Regardless of cooking style, the most important lessons Hugh has taught me are respect for quality ingredients, building a relationship with local farmers, and leading your staff by example."

LAMB MEATBALLS
WITH DRIED CHERRY SAUCE
Yields about 24 meatballs

- 2 cups dried sour cherries
- 2 cups hot water
- 2 pounds lamb, ground
- 1 teaspoon allspice, ground
- 1 teaspoon cinnamon, ground
- 1 teaspoon coriander, ground
- 1 teaspoon cumin, ground
- 2-1/2 teaspoons kosher salt
- 1/2 teaspoon pepper, freshly ground
- 1/4 cup & 1 tablespoon olive oil
- 2 medium onions, coarsely chopped
- 3 tablespoons fresh lemon juice
- 2 tablespoons flat-leaf parsley leaves
- 2 tablespoons pine nuts

In a bowl, soak dried cherries in the hot water until softened, about 30 minutes.

In a large bowl, spread the lamb in an even layer. In a small bowl, combine the spices, salt, and pepper. Sprinkle the mixture over the lamb and knead. Form the lamb into 1-inch meatballs; you should have about 24. In a large skillet, heat 2 tablespoons of olive oil until simmering. Working in batches, add the meatballs and cook over medium-high heat. Cook until lightly browned outside and rare in the center, about 4 minutes. Reserve. In a large saucepan, heat the remaining 3 tablespoons of olive oil. Add the onions and cook over moderately low heat, stirring occasionally, until softened and golden, about 12 minutes. Add the cherries and their soaking liquid and the lemon juice and simmer over moderate heat for 10 minutes. Pulse the cherry sauce in a blender until pureed but not smooth. Return the sauce to the pan. Add the meatballs and any accumulated juices and simmer over low heat until they are slightly pink inside and the sauce has reduced slightly, 5 to 10 minutes. Season with salt and pepper. Garnish with parsley and pine nuts. Wonderful alone or serve with warm bread of choice! We recommend a soft, chewy pita.

CUCUMBER GAZPACHO

Serves 2 to 4

- 6 cups cucumbers, peeled, seeded and chopped (The National uses the longer European variety)
- 1 cup good-quality extra virgin olive oil (This is important. Use the best oil you can. It really makes a difference.)
- 3/4 cup ice water
- 1 clove garlic, minced
- 1/4 cup white wine vinegar
- 1 tablespoon lemon juice
- 1-1/2 teaspoons kosher salt
- 1/4 teaspoon ground black pepper
- Pinch ground cayenne pepper

Combine ingredients and puree in a blender in batches until very smooth. Serve well chilled. Each batch of cucumbers will be slightly different. As a result, you will probably need to tweak the soup with more oil, more salt, more vinegar, and/or lemon juice, etc. until it's just the way you want it. At the restaurant, the dish is garnished with radishes and croutons.

THE NATIONAL TONIC

Serves 1

- Fill a pint glass with ice and add:
- 2 ounces Bulleit Bourbon
- Juice of 1/2 grapefruit, about 3 ounces
- Top with Blenheim spicy ginger ale, about 3 ounces

The unofficial cocktail of Athens is Bulleit Bourbon, spicy ginger ale, and lemon. We're not sure where it started, but The National's interpretation is this refreshing beverage. They favor Bulleit Kentucky bourbon at the restaurant with spicy ginger ale made by Blenheim in South Carolina and the juice of a freshly squeezed grapefruit (ruby red if you can get it). Serve it over ice in a pint glass. Whether you've just worked a shift in the kitchen, are heading to a show at the 40 Watt, or going to watch the Dawgs, it's the perfect tonic to get things started or slow things down.

THE PINE

1235 S. Milledge Avenue
Athens, GA 30606
(706) 208-0059

www.thepineathens.com

SCOTT PARRISH & SACHIN PATEL • OWNERS
JARAD BLANTON • CHEF

The Pine, a locally owned pub in the heart of historic Five Points, offers an authentic yet innovative Southern menu, which includes savory favorites such as pimento cheese crostini with bacon marmalade, fresh cornbread, a creative deviled-egg trio, and wood-fired flatbreads. Their all-American beverage program specializes in craft beers, whiskeys, and wines. The Pine's festive monthly wine tastings and daily menu specials have become a go-to staple for many locals.

Co-owner Scott Parrish has lived in Athens for nearly twenty years and is proud to call Athens home. After moving to Athens to attend the University of Georgia, Scott landed a job at Athens Country Club, quickly moving his way up to an assistant clubhouse manager and beverage director position. After eight years, Scott moved on to be a fine wine sales consultant guiding many independent restaurants in Athens through his elite wine program. After nine years in the wine world, Scott decided it was his time to set up his own shop. Scott and his business partner, Sachin Patel, opened up The Pine in May of 2014 and haven't looked back since.

Chef Jarad Blanton is an Athens culinary veteran. He has been responsible for cooking up tasty dishes at local favorites, such as The National, 5 & 10, and East West Bistro. Although he comes from a very traditional Southern upbringing, Chef Blanton has fostered his sophisticated inspiration from a worldly culinary perspective. Asian flavors are a particular favorite and are clearly pronounced in his dishes, such as his interpretation of the classic Korean steam bun.

HOISIN BRAISED PORK SHOULDER

Serves 8 to 10

- 1 5-pound boneless pork shoulder
- 2 cups hoisin sauce
- 6 cloves fresh garlic, peeled and crushed
- 1 knob fresh ginger, peeled and sliced
- 1/2 cup Sambal Oelek chili paste
- Juice & zest of 1 lime
- Juice & zest of 1 orange
- 1 quart chicken stock
- 2 quarts Cheerwine

Remove fat cap from shoulder and cut pork into 3-by-3-inch cubes. Brown the pork on all sides in vegetable oil in a Dutch oven. Remove pork and add garlic and ginger to the oil and sauté until golden brown. Pour off excess oil and deglaze Dutch oven with chicken stock. Add pork back to Dutch oven and add in all remaining ingredients, gently rolling around the pork to evenly disperse all ingredients. Cover and place in 375°F preheated oven and braise for 4 hours. Allow pork to cool and remove from Dutch oven. Strain liquid through a fine sieve to remove all debris. Pull pork apart with a fork until shredded.

MISO SOY PICKLES
Serves 4 to 8, depending on use

- 2 large seedless cucumbers
- 2 cups rice wine vinegar
- 1 cup soy sauce
- 1 cup mirin
- 1/2 cup brown sugar
- 1/2 cup red miso paste

Wash and slice cucumbers thinly but do not peel. Combine all other ingredients and stir while bringing to a boil. Pour boiling liquid over sliced cucumbers. Allow cooling and refrigerating overnight. Excellent on sandwiches.

SWEET CHILI MAYO
Yields about 2 cups

- 1 cup Duke's Mayonnaise
- 1 cup Mae Ploy sweet chili sauce
- 1 teaspoon Sriracha

Mix all ingredients well and serve. Perfect as a dip and on sandwiches.

THE ROYAL PEASANT

1675 S. Lumpkin Street
Athens, GA 30606
(706) 549-7920

www.royalpeasant.com

MICHAEL WHITE • OWNER
LUKE ROBERT HARVEY • CHEF

The Royal Peasant is nestled snugly in the beloved Five Points neighborhood, drawing Athenians with its magnetic charm reminiscent of a quaint English gastropub. The menu features traditional British fare with a modern twist, often showcasing a dash of Indian influence. This simple but thoughtful menu features dishes like house-made chips and lamb stew, bangers and mash, and, of course, freshly fried fish and chips. The bar scene is always a good time, filled to the brim with lively patrons watching their favorite football (American soccer) teams and enjoying a tasty craft brew.

Chef Luke Harvey was born in Springfield, Missouri, and moved to the Classic City to study biology at the University of Georgia. After college, he found his love for cooking while running the kitchen at Porterhouse Grill. After a few years at Porterhouse, he transitioned into his current position as the executive chef at The Royal Peasant. Chef Harvey serves up inviting, traditional pub fare as well as adventurous dishes showcasing Thai and Indian influences, such as his impressive Smoked Chicken Curry.

SHEPHERD'S PIE

Serves 4 to 6

- · 2-1/2 pounds ground lamb (substitute ground beef if desired)
- · 1 red onion, diced
- · 1 shallot, diced
- · 2 garlic cloves, peeled and minced
- · 1 whole carrot, diced
- · 1 whole parsnip, diced
- · 1 cup chopped oyster or crimini mushrooms
- · 1/2 teaspoon of each of the following, finely minced: rosemary, tarragon, and thyme
- · 1 teaspoon tomato paste
- · 1/2 cup olive oil
- · 4 ounces frozen green peas
- · 4 Yukon Gold potatoes, peeled
- · 1/2 cup panko bread crumbs
- · 1/4 cup goat cheese (substitute sharp white cheddar if desired)
- · Kosher salt to taste

Boil the potatoes in lightly salted water until soft. Mash and stir in goat cheese. Season to taste with kosher salt and set aside. Preheat oven to 375°F.

Heat olive oil and brown the ground lamb. Scoop out the meat with a slotted spoon and set aside. Return the pot to medium-high heat and sauté herbs, vegetables, and tomato paste until soft. Mix lamb, green peas, and sautéed vegetables. Grease the sides and bottom of a 9-by-13-inch baking dish and spread the mixture evenly throughout. Using a rubber spatula evenly spread the potato mixture over top. Finish with panko bread crumbs. Bake at 375°F for 15 to 20 minutes until crisp and golden brown on top.

STICKY TOFFEE PUDDING

Serves 4 to 6

- 2 cups pitted dates
- 4 Earl Grey tea bags
- 2-1/2 cups water
- 1-1/2 cups all-purpose flour
- 1 teaspoon baking powder
- 3/4 cup room temperature butter, unsalted
- 2 cups cane sugar
- 1 teaspoon vanilla extract
- 1/2 teaspoon kosher salt
- 6 eggs, beaten

Preheat oven to 425°F. Steep dates and Earl Grey in water for 7 minutes. Remove dates (keep the liquid) and allow them to cool for 5 minutes before pureeing in a food processer. Using an electric mixer, whip butter, sugar, salt, baking powder, and vanilla extract together until smooth. Gradually add all-purpose flour until batter is smooth and free of lumps. Blend tea liquid and pureed dates into the batter. Blend in beaten eggs. Grease sides and bottom of a 9-by-13-inch baking dish, pour in batter, and bake for 30 minutes at 425°F.

Chef's Note: Enjoy with a big scoop of vanilla gelato or caramel sauce and shaved dark chocolate.

BANGERS AND MASH

Serves 4

- · 4 high-quality pork sausages
- · 1 head savoy cabbage
- · 1 head Swiss chard
- · 1 shallot, julienned
- · 8 Yukon Gold potatoes, peeled
- · 1/4 cup red wine vinegar
- · 1 teaspoon smoked paprika
- · 1 teaspoon cumin
- · 1 teaspoon turmeric
- · 1 teaspoon ancho chili powder
- · 3 cups chicken stock
- · 2 teaspoons Worcestershire sauce
- · 2 teaspoons kosher salt
- · 1 teaspoon cane sugar
- · 2 teaspoons tomato paste
- · 1/4 cup olive oil
- · 1 teaspoon unsalted butter

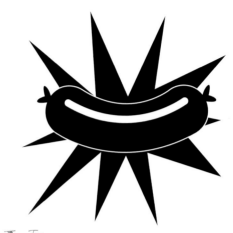

Why are sausages called bangers? *During the First World War, meat was scarce and sausage contained very little actual meat. Instead, grains, cheap meat scraps, and water were used to fill out the sausages. When they were fried, they would sputter and make small banging sounds.*

Preheat oven to 375°F. Bring chicken stock to a simmer over medium heat and whisk in tomato paste, sugar, vinegar, salt, smoked paprika, cumin, Worcestershire sauce, and ancho chili powder. Simmer for 15 minutes and set sauce aside. Boil potatoes in lightly-salted water until soft. Whip until smooth with unsalted butter and season to taste with kosher salt and set aside. Cut cabbage and Swiss chard into thin strips. Sauté with julienned shallots, olive oil, and turmeric while sausages are browning in the oven. Cook sausages on 375°F until cooked through and the skin is crisp. Ladle sauce onto four plates, add a scoop of potatoes and a crispy sausage to each, and finish with sautéed turmeric cabbage.

SEABEAR OYSTER BAR

297 Prince Avenue Suite 10
Athens, GA 30601
(706) 850-4367

www.seabearoysterbar.com

PATRICK STUBBERS • CHEF / CO-OWNER

Chef Patrick Stubbers fostered an early interest in the culinary arts while in college and, after relocating to Athens, continued to sharpen his skills working in and around the kitchen at The Grit, another local Athens favorite. Starting as a dishwasher, he steadily worked his way through the ranks and was quickly promoted to manager. It was his experience cooking The Grit's innovative vegetarian menus that helped nurture his growth as a chef. He went on to help found The Fourcoursemen, a supper club that doubled as a delicious hobby for foodie enthusiasts. As the group's culinary abilities grew, so did their reputation. Eventually, due to the club's popularity, The Fourcoursemen landed a television show, one episode of which was even nominated for a James Beard Award!

Chef Peter Dale, who at the time had been in the process of opening up his new restaurant, The National, enthusiastically brought Patrick aboard as his executive sous chef. The two have spent the last seven plus years working together and exploring the country, constantly looking to expand their knowledge of all things food. These experiences, combined with a mutual love for inventive seafood dishes, casual bar fare, and creative cocktails, inspired the idea for Seabear Oyster Bar. Bonus: They have the only absinthe drip in town!

SEABEAR CLASSIC CLAM CHOWDER

Serves 6 to 8

- 1/2 cup butter
- 1 cup Vidalia or yellow onions, small dice
- 2 celery stalks, diced
- 4 ounces pancetta, diced (or bacon)
- 3/4 teaspoons Old Bay Seasoning
- 1/4 cup white wine
- 3 cups milk
- 1-1/2 cups heavy cream
- 1 cup clam juice
- 1-3/4 pounds russet potatoes, diced
- 2 bay leaves
- 4 teaspoons dry sherry
- 4 teaspoons Texas Pete Original Hot Sauce
- 4 teaspoons Worcestershire
- 8 ounces clam meat
- 4 teaspoons parsley, chopped
- 4 teaspoons chives, thinly sliced
- Kosher salt & pepper, to taste

Place the butter, onion, celery, pancetta, and Old Bay in a large soup pot over medium heat. Sauté until onions are translucent. Add wine, milk, 1/2 cup of heavy cream, clam juice, potatoes, bay leaves, sherry, Texas Pete, and Worcestershire. Simmer until potatoes are soft, just before edges break. In a blender, puree 1/3 of the soup, and then return to the rest of the soup.

To serve, add clams, remaining heavy cream, parsley, and chives. Heat soup until piping hot. Season to taste with salt and pepper. Serve immediately.

SHRIMP & CRAB CAKES

Serves 4 to 6

- 6 tablespoons unsalted butter
- 1/4 cup & 2 tablespoons olive oil
- 3/4 cup red onion, diced
- 1-1/2 cups celery, diced
- 1/2 cup red bell pepper, diced
- 1/2 cup green bell pepper, diced
- 1/4 cup fresh flat-leaf parsley, minced
- 1 tablespoon capers, drained
- 1/4 teaspoon Texas Pete Original Hot Sauce
- 1/2 teaspoon Worcestershire
- 1-1/2 teaspoons Old Bay Seasoning
- 1/2 teaspoon kosher salt
- 1/2 teaspoon ground black pepper
- 1/4 pound cooked shrimp, chopped
- 1/4 pound lump crabmeat, picked and drained
- 2 large eggs, lightly beaten
- 1/2 cup breadcrumbs
- 1/2 cup Duke's Mayonnaise
- 2 teaspoons Dijon mustard

Place 2 tablespoons of butter, 2 tablespoons of oil, onion, celery, red and green bell peppers, parsley, capers, Texas Pete, Worcestershire, Old Bay, salt, and pepper in a large sauté pan over medium-low heat and cook until the vegetables are soft, approximately 15 to 20 minutes. Cool to room temperature. In a large bowl, combine the shrimp, crab, breadcrumbs, mayonnaise, mustard, and eggs. Add the cooked mixture and mix well. Cover and chill in the refrigerator for 1 hour. When cool, form into desired shape and size.

Heat the remaining butter and olive oil for frying over medium heat in a large sauté pan. Add the cakes and fry for 4 to 5 minutes on each side, until browned. Serve right away with remoulade or tartar sauce.

SPEAKEASY

269 E. Broad Street
Athens, GA 30601
(706) 546-5556

www.speakeasyathens.com

PATRICK ANDERSON • EXECUTIVE CHEF / OWNER

For over thirteen years, Speakeasy was an all-time favorite in Athens. During the production of this book, chef and owner Patrick Anderson moved on, and Speakeasy permanently closed its doors. Two of their house favorite recipes will now live on thanks to Pat's contribution to *Classic City Cooking*.

Located in beautiful Downtown Athens, Speakeasy overlooked historic East Broad Street. With an eclectic menu concentrating mainly on Southern-inspired tapas, their tasty small plates provided for an intimate setting shared amongst friends. Speakeasy offered a wide selection from its award-winning wine list, not to mention their creatively inspired cocktails and delectable handcrafted desserts. While in college, Speakeasy became a frequented favorite of my friends and mine. It was the perfect place to go with a group and order a little bit of everything, as long as you were okay with sharing!

Chef Patrick Anderson started at Speakeasy as executive chef in 2002, when the restaurant first opened. Patrick's pure love for food, in addition to his desire to mold his own culinary destiny, led him to purchase Speakeasy from the original owners in 2004. Pat and his recipes leave big shoes to fill for the next up-and-coming Athens restaurant. Thank you, Speakeasy, for the incredible food and a host of good times.

SUGAR COOKIES
WITH CREAM CHEESE FROSTING
Yields 15 to 20 cookies

- 1/2 pound butter
- 3 cups flour
- 2 cups sugar
- 2 eggs
- 1 teaspoon vanilla
- 1/2 teaspoon baking soda
- 1 teaspoon cream of tartar
- Cream Cheese Frosting (recipe included)
- Maraschino cherries

Soften butter and place in mixing bowl. Work in flour and sugar until mixture resembles rough cornmeal. In a separate bowl, whisk eggs, vanilla, soda, and cream of tartar. Add wet ingredients to the dry bowl and mix until well incorporated. Do not over mix. Store in refrigerator overnight. Form into 1-ounce balls, roll in sugar, flatten, and bake on a greased cookie sheet in preheated 350°F oven for 8 to 10 minutes or until edges begin to brown. Remove from oven, cool on rack, and serve with Cream Cheese Frosting and maraschino cherries.

CREAM CHEESE FROSTING

- 8 ounces cream cheese
- 3 teaspoons whole milk
- 1 teaspoon vanilla
- 6 tablespoons 10X sugar

Soften cheese. Combine all ingredients in food processor or blender. Blend until smooth. Add more milk if too thick.

Chef's Note: Serve with a big, tall glass of milk or hot chocolate!

WARM SPINACH DIP

Serves 4 to 6

- · 1/2 pound butter
- · 1 cup flour
- · 4 cups whole milk
- · 3/4 cup Parmesan, shredded
- · 1/4 cup feta, crumbled
- · 1/2 teaspoon crushed red pepper
- · 1 pound fresh spinach, chopped
- · 1 honey wheat bread bowl (optional)
- · Kosher salt & pepper, to taste

In large pot, melt butter and add flour, stirring 2 minutes until starch cooks but does not brown. Add milk slowly, bring to a simmer and stir until sauce thickens. Add cheeses, salt and pepper to taste, and crushed red pepper. Stir until well incorporated. Remove from heat, add spinach, and stir well. Serve warm in honey wheat bread bowl or with toasted honey wheat bread (or bread of choice). Also great with veggies!

VIVA! ARGENTINE CUISINE

**247 Prince Avenue
Athens, GA 30601
(706) 850-8284**

www.vivaargentinecuisine.com

GABY LINDSEY, JESSE LINDSEY • CHEFS / OWNERS

Chef Gaby Lindsey cultivated her love for cooking at a very young age under the tutelage of her beloved mother, Elena Krapf. Having grown up in Buenos Aires, Argentina, Elena moved to United States when she was sixteen years old with an extensive knowledge and passion for Argentinian home cooking. Throughout their lives together, Gaby and her mother often spoke about one day opening a restaurant together and sharing this passion with others.

Their dream was realized in 2011, when Gaby, with the unwavering help and support of her family, opened Viva!'s doors for the first time and began sharing her heritage with the people of Athens. Although Gaby's mother passed away in 2005, Elena's loving presence is felt in every aspect of Viva!'s culinary character, including the framed picture of her sitting next to the cash register.

Speaking as a native Athenian, I can truly say that Viva!'s delicious menu has made—and continues to make—an important contribution to the Classic City's tradition of artful expression and authenticity. Over the years, Gaby has been able to cultivate quite a following for her unique style of Argentine cooking, not the least of which with her famous cupcakes. Sadly for us, she strongly insists the recipe for these cupcakes remain a secret—they are, after all, a sacred family tradition—so I guess you'll just have to go in and try one yourself. Word on the street is that her Dulce de Leche and Salted Peanut Butter Mousse will change your life!

TRADITIONAL GROUND BEEF EMPANADAS

Serves 4 to 6 (8 empanadas)

- · 1 pound ground beef
- · 1 tablespoon House Seasoning (recipe included)
- · 1 teaspoon paprika
- · 1 tablespoon Worcestershire sauce
- · 1 hardboiled egg, minced
- · 4 green onions, chopped
- · 1/4 cup green olive, chopped
- · Pinch red pepper flake
- · 1 teaspoon red wine vinegar

HOUSE SEASONING

- · 1 cup kosher salt
- · 1 tablespoon garlic powder
- · 1 tablespoon freshly-cracked pepper

Cook beef in a hot skillet until browned.* Drain off fat, leaving 1 tablespoon in pan.

Add remaining ingredients, stir, and cool completely. Make or buy empanada discs (Goya makes a great product, available in a lot of grocers' freezer sections!).

Roll out empanada discs to 6-inch rounds. Moisten edge with water. Put 2 to 3 tablespoons of mixture in center of disc, fold over and crimp or fork edges.

Fry at 375°F for 3 minutes.

Gaby's mom used lard. Canola oil is used at the restaurant . . . feel free to use either!

BUTTERNUT SQUASH BISQUE

Serves 4

- · 2 tablespoons extra virgin olive oil
- · 2 small yellow onions, minced
- · 3 cups butternut squash, peeled, seeded, and cubed
- · 5 cups vegetable stock (store-bought or homemade)
- · 1-1/2 cups red potatoes, peeled and cubed
- · 1 teaspoon paprika
- · 1 tablespoon white table sugar
- · 1/2 cup heavy cream
- · 4 teaspoons chives, minced for garnish

Heat extra virgin olive oil in large saucepan. Add onion and cook until soft, about 5 to 6 minutes.

Add squash, stock, potatoes, paprika, and sugar. Boil, reduce heat to low, cover, and simmer about 35 minutes or until vegetables are soft. Use immersion blender and blend until smooth. Stir in cream. Re-season and reheat if needed. Ladle into soup bowls and garnish with minced chives.

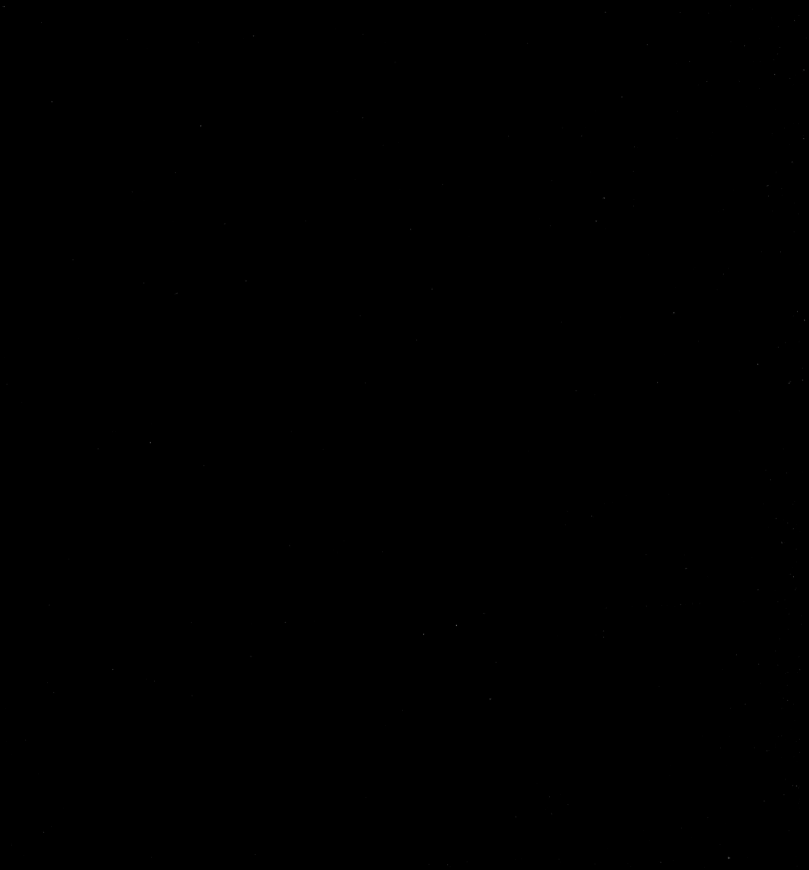

HONORABLE MENTIONS

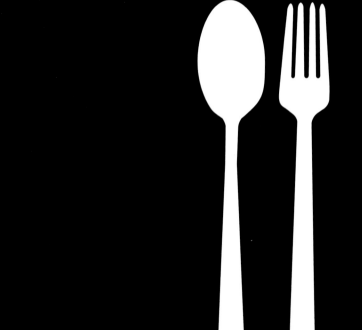

STILL HUNGRY? THERE'S MORE ...

Athens is so full of culinary magic; we felt an honorable mentions list was necessary. From Korean to French to Spanish cuisine, below you will find a list of equally amazing restaurants and the must-order items you need to try. Take note and eat up!

AGUA LINDA
A family-owned and operated Mexican restaurant with two convenient locations in Athens.

1376 Prince Avenue
Athens, GA 30606
(706) 543-1500

2080 Timothy Road
Athens, GA 30606
(706) 543-0154

Must-Try Items: The cheese dip. It's not quite "authentic" Mexican as it's actually made with American cheese, but it's the greatest tortilla chip accompaniment EVER. Get the dip. They also make the best Tex-Mex dirty margarita!

AUTOMATIC PIZZA
Townie paradise located in the heart of Normaltown. This hip pizza joint has hand-tossed pizzas with fresh, organic ingredients.

1397 Prince Avenue
Athens, GA 30606
(706) 850-2037

Must-Try Items: A large, cheesy pie to share. The Smoked Chicken Parmesan Sandwich and a cannoli should also do the trick!

BLIND PIG TAVERN
A classic gathering spot for trivia, live music, game days, and endless pitchers of your favorite beer.

312 E. Washington Street
Athens, GA 30605
(706) 548-3442

Must-Try Items: The Fried Mushrooms with House-made Ranch Sauce and a Burger with Caramelized Onions on your style bun is a great place to start.

CALI-N-TITO'S
Unique Latin American eats. BYOB.

1427 S. Lumpkin Street
Athens, GA 30605
(706) 227-9979

Must-Try Items: Fish Tacos, El Sandwich Cubano (not your traditional Cuban sandwich, but tasty), and Fried Plantains. Bring cash and lots of beer.

CECILIA VILLAVECES CAKES
A family-owned specialty bakery baking the very best layer cakes in town.

610 N. Milledge Avenue
Athens, GA 30601
(706) 543-3308

Must-Try Items: All the cakes are spectacular. The Triple Leche with strawberries is their masterpiece. The Hummingbird, Red Velvet, and Carrot Cakes are also among the most popular. Order in advance. The cakes can also be found at featured restaurant Last Resort Grill.

CLOCKED

A diner located next to the 40 Watt, cooking up organic, local comfort food and out-of-this-world burgers and fries.

259 W. Washington Street
Athens, GA 30601
(706) 548-9175

Must-Try Items: Blackberry Bacon Jam Burger, Vegan Slaw, and Cheese Fries.

CONDOR CHOCOLATES

A chocolate factory and café owned by local brothers, Nick and The National Chef/Owner, Peter Dale.

1658 S. Lumpkin Street
Athens, GA 30606
(706) 850-4803

Must-Try Items: Dark Chocolate and Smoked Sea Salt Bar and every single truffle on the menu. The Honey Lavender is particularly interesting as well as mind-blowing.

ETIENNE

A relaxed French bistro with creative cocktails and all of your classic French favorites.

311 E. Broad Street
Athens, GA 30601
(706) 850-8008

Must-Try Items: Steak Frites and the Coq Au Vin. Complete your meal with an order of their Crème Brulee and/or the House-made Chocolate Limoncello.

FOOD FOR THE SOUL

Authentic Southern soul food served in a no-frills setting.

1965 W. Broad Street
Athens, GA 30606
(706) 546-0052

Must-Try Items: Fried Pork Chop, Cheese and Broccoli Rice, Mac and Cheese, and their Fried Okra. Banana Pudding for dessert is an obvious choice and a glass of sweet tea is a given.

GEORGIA THEATRE

This landmark venue has helped launch the careers of bands such as R.E.M., Widespread Panic, and The Whigs. A recent renovation included a new rooftop bar and kitchen, serving up tasty snacks and bar food.

215 N. Lumpkin Street
Athens, GA 30601
(706) 850-7670

Must-Try Items: Spicy Pimento Cheese, Fried Chicken Skins, and the Grass-fed Burger should do it. Veggie lovers can enjoy Smoked Tofu Tacos and Veggie Banh Mi. All of the above will pair perfectly with a cold brew.

THE GLOBE

A classic casual bar recently voted one of the best pubs in the country by *Esquire* and located in the heart of the Classic City. An excellent selection of food and beverage along with a hip, local vibe attracts locals and visitors on a daily basis.

199 N. Lumpkin Street
Athens, GA 30601
(706) 353-4721

Must-Try Items: Start with the Globe Nachos and a local brew. If you're really hungry, give the Burger or the Fish and Chips a try. Try to make it for happy hour and you may get lucky with a complimentary bread and cheese plate.

THE GRILL

A laid-back American diner open all day, every day.

171 College Avenue
Athens, GA 30601
(706) 543-4770

Must-Try Items: French Fries with Feta Dressing and a Chocolate Milkshake. Perfect for a late-night bite.

THE GRIT

A veggie lover's paradise. A 100% meat-free eatery in one of Athens's most historic buildings, serving up innovative vegetarian/vegan dishes.

199 Prince Avenue
Athens, GA 30601
(706) 543-6592

Must-Try Items: The Loaded Nachos are a perfect start. Go with the Veggie Plate so you can mix and match. The signature Golden Bowl is also a solid choice.

IDEAL BAGEL

Fresh homemade bagels with signature spreads & fresh fish options.

815 W. Broad Street
Athens, GA 30601
(706) 353-0005

Must-Try Items: The Tupelo, Everything Bagel with Lox, and the Bacon-Tomato and Espresso Cream Cheeses.

IKE & JANE

Café and bakery serving both breakfast and lunch with made-from-scratch goodies.

1307 Prince Avenue
Athens, GA 30606
(706) 850-1580

Must Try Items: The Elvis!, Fruity Pebbles Doughnut (all the doughnuts are winners), and the Peanut Butter and Nutella Sandwich … so what if it's on the kids menu?

INDEPENDENT BAKING CO.

A bread and breakfast pastry bakery. Everything on the menu is made from scratch on premises and baked fresh daily.

1625 S. Lumpkin Street
Athens, GA 30606
(706) 850-3550

Must-Try Items: Melt-in-your-mouth Croissants, Pain Au Chocolat, Morning Roll, and the Classic Baguette. Grab a cappuccino for the road.

IRON FACTORY

Savory Korean BBQ complete with private karaoke rooms.

255 W. Washington Street
Athens, GA 30601
(706) 395-6877

Must-Try Items: The Pork Belly and Kimchi Rice. You're welcome. Stay for a little late-night karaoke.

JUST PHO

Vietnamese cuisine specializing in noodle soups and sandwiches.

1063 Baxter Steet #100
Athens, GA 30606
(706) 850-1420

Must-Try Items: Pho Thai, Avocado Smoothie, BBQ Banh Mi. Enjoy a cup of their Vietnamese coffee before or after your meal.

KELLY'S JERK

Jamaican food with a Southern twist.

1583 S. Lumpkin Street
Athens, GA 30605
(706) 208-0000

Must-Try Items: Jerk Pork, Spicy Cabbage, Mac and Cheese, and Cornbread. Guzzle a tall glass of their homemade sweet tea to tame the flavors.

LA DOLCE VITA

Red Sauce Italian served in a comfortable yet intimate setting.

323 E. Broad Street
Athens, GA 30601
(706) 353-3911

Must-Try Items: Bruschetta, Carpaccio, Gnocchi alla Sorrentina, and Lasagna al Forno. Perfect for date night.

LOS AMIGOS

A Mexican grocery store serving up cheap, delicious tacos.

109 Rowe Road
Athens, GA 30601
(706) 543-9637

Must-Try Items: There are only about five tacos on the menu, each of which will cost you about a buck. Order them all.

MARKER 7

A lively coastal grill with a stunning patio overlooking Athens's Historic Five Points.

1195 S. Milledge Avenue
Athens, GA 30605
(706) 850-3451

Must-Try Items: Enjoy the Grouper Nuggets, Shrimp and Grits, and Hushpuppies on the patio!

PORTERHOUSE

A casual steakhouse offering classic meals and Sunday brunch buffet.

459 E. Broad Street
Athens, GA 30601
(706) 369-0990

Must-Try Items: The entire brunch buffet, She-Crab Soup, Prime Rib, and Seafood Tortellini.

PULASKI HEIGHTS BBQ

BYOB BBQ joint serving everything from wings to stews to meats by the pound.

675 Pulaski Street #100
Athens, GA 30601
(706) 583-9600

Must-Try Items: Deviled Eggs, Redneck Reuben, Squash Casserole, and Pulled Pork. Get the "Family Dinner" for a tasty bargain.

SHOKITINI

A local Japanese restaurant featuring hibachi entrees, sushi rolls, and sake.

251 W. Clayton Street #117
Athens, GA 30601
(706) 353-7933

Must-Try Items: Miso Soup, Red & Black Roll, Game Day Roll, and Seaweed Salad. Bonus: private karaoke rooms!

TACO STAND

A longtime local staple serving cheap Mexican eats, beer, and a full bar.

247 E. Broad Street
Athens, GA 30601
(706) 549-1446

670 N. Milledge Avenue
Athens, GA 30601
(706) 549-2894

2230 Barnett Shoals Road
Athens, GA 30605
(706) 549-5481

Must-Try Items: Cheese Dip, BBQ Tacos, Mega Burrito, and margaritas.

THAI SPOON

Fresh dumplings, curry, and other classic Thai dishes within stumbling distance to the Georgia Theatre.

149 N. Lumpkin Street
Athens, GA 30601
(706) 548-9222

Must-Try Items: The Massaman Curry is an absolute must, as is the Chicken Larb Salad.

THE VARSITY

No list in regards to the Classic City would be complete without The Varsity. After opening in 1932, this Athens institution has been serving up their famous chilidogs and deliciously greasy fried onion rings to visitors and locals alike.

1000 W. Broad Street
Athens GA 30606
(706) 548-6325

Must-Try Items: The aforementioned Chilidogs and Onion Rings of course! A Frosted Orange is a major must, as are the Fried Pies. One pseudo "healthy" note: all fried items are cooked in pure rice bran oil, which is low in saturated fat and contains no cholesterol or trans fats. Well then, "What'll ya have?"

WORLD FAMOUS

Hip music venue serving up Southern eats, craft beers, and signature cocktails.

351 N. Hull Street
Athens, GA 30601
(706) 543-4002

Must-Try Items: Fried Chicken and Waffle Club (a MUST!), fried green tomatoes, and the Bojack's Belmont Jewel cocktail.

Do you need coffee in your life to function? We understand. Athens just happens to have two specialty roasters at your service. Long standing favorite Jittery Joe's Coffee just celebrated twenty-one years of business, and 1000 Faces Coffee touched down in 2006 and focuses on a free trade, sustainable coffee culture. Take your pick!

Makers
&
Shapers

BILLY BENNETT
Former University of Georgia Football Kicker

photo courtesy of Billy Bennett

One thing we know for sure about Athens, Georgia—they love football! Bennett is one of the most decorated place kickers in Georgia history. He had thirteen Georgia records, nine SEC records, and seven NCAA records when his playing career ended in 2003. Before going to Georgia, he was an All-State kicker at Athens Academy and booted a school-record 54-yard field goal in 1999.

Billy was born in Athens in 1982, a time when University of Georgia football was in its glory days and Athens's legendary college rock music scene was just beginning to blossom, which would possibly explain how twenty years later he ended up both playing football for the University of Georgia (2000-2003) and helping local bands like The Whigs and Dead Confederate make their first records. He's currently in Nashville, still a Bulldawg fan, of course, and making records as always. He still gets home to Athens a few times a year to see his folks and catch a football game or live show.

What's your favorite restaurant in Athens and why?
I've always loved Last Resort. Worth the price of admission alone for the Vidalia Bacon dressing, it's always my go-to for a date night or celebration. It also has an excellent Sunday brunch, not to mention it was quite the late-night hot spot in college while I was at UGA.

If you could eat one dish out in Athens before you die, what would it be?
Taco Stand [on Milledge]. The number 5, peppers, no onions, hot sauce on the side, with a Dr. Pepper and a small cheese dip.

If you could plan your perfect day/night out in Athens, what would you do and who would you do it with?
Hmmmmm, nothing fancy here. Great dinner with friends (maybe at The National), catch a big show at the Georgia Theatre, and hang later at The Globe or Manhattan.

What Athens celebrity, dead or alive, would you want to grab drinks with? Why?
Well, I'm sober, so no one—ha! Just kidding. I don't get that starstruck, but maybe I would have a cranberry and OJ with Sky from Nowhere Bar 'cause I never got to tell that dude goodbye.

Who's your favorite celebrity chef?
Gotta say Hugh, right?

If you could hop on a plane and go anywhere in the world for dinner, where would you go? What restaurant?
Cinque Terra, Italy—green trofie pasta was the best I've ever had.

DARIUS GOES WEST

An Award-Winning Documentary Created by Athens Locals

photo courtesy of *Darius Goes West*

B oth Darius Weems and movie producer Logan Smalley created the award-winning and well-known documentary, *Darius Goes West*, as a means of creating awareness about Duchenne Muscular Dystrophy—a fatal disease claiming thousands of children's lives every year.

In this multi-award-winning documentary, fifteen-year-old Darius Weems and eleven of his best friends set off across America with the ultimate goal of getting his wheelchair customized on MTV's *Pimp My Ride*. The result is a rarely seen testament to the explosive idealism of today's youth, as well as a vivid portrayal of adventure, of brotherhood, and of the character and strength it takes to shed light on an uncertain future. Not only does Darius bravely face his own inevitable fate with Duchenne Muscular Dystrophy (DMD), but through his unflinching humor and his extraordinary laugh, he sparks a revolution in the lives of everyone who crosses—and then shares—his courageous path.

I'd love to have a drink with Herschel Walker. I'm a big Georgia Bulldawg fan, and he's a legend.

Darius Weems:

What Athens celebrity, dead or alive, would you want to grab drinks with? Why?

I'd love to have a drink with Herschel Walker. I'm a big Georgia Bulldawg fan, and he's a legend. I think we'd have a lot of fun talking sports.

Who's your favorite celebrity chef?

My stepdad, Tommy Davis. Nobody cooks up chicken and ribs on the grill like he does.

If you could only pick one Athens restaurant to go to, which one would you choose?

I like Porterhouse Grill. The food is fresh, the steaks are always cooked perfectly, and the manager there always recognizes me, says hello, and comes over to the table and asks me how I'm doing.

If you could hop on a plane and go anywhere in the world for dinner, where would you go? What restaurant?

Brennan's in New Orleans. We had breakfast there when we were filming *Darius Goes West*, and it was amazing.

Logan Smalley:

A graduate of Clarke Central High School and the University of Georgia, Smalley is the director of the award-winning documentary and nonprofit organization, *Darius Goes West*. Though frequently in Athens, he currently resides in New York City where he serves as Director of TED Conferences' official educational initiative, TED-Ed. The website has won three Webby Awards and is used by millions of students and teachers around the world. Most recently, Logan, along with a few *Darius Goes West* crew members, founded a unique online book discovery engine called "Call Me Ishmael." The website, which is based on the famous opening line of *Moby Dick*, allows bibliophiles to "call Ishmael" on a phone and to leave him a message about a book that changed their life.

If you could eat one dish out in Athens before you die, what would it be?
A milkshake from The Grill. Yes, they count as an entire meal. It's not news that they're delicious, but being from Athens gives them a certain sentimental value. I've had Grill milkshakes with all of my favorite Athenians. That said, don't ask me to share.

Who's your favorite celebrity chef?
This is a tough one for me, as I don't have cable television, but I consider Mike Waldrip (father of friend Nick Waldrip) to be a celebrity chef. It's unlikely he has been on TV, but Nick and I have made it our personal mission to share his homemade BBQ sauce with random New Yorkers, and I'm happy to report that he is officially famous within a five-block radius.

If you could hop on a plane and go anywhere in the world for dinner, where would you go? What restaurant?
I once had a rack of lamb in Jackson Hole, Wyoming, that made me want to move there. In fact, I did move there for a summer, and during that time I saw more of a restaurant called The Blue Lion than I did the Teton Mountains. Get the rack of lamb, even if you don't like rack of lamb.

DRIVE-BY TRUCKERS

Boasting a mix of Southern pride, erudite lyrics, and a muscled three-guitar attack, Athens-based Drive-By Truckers became one of the most well respected alternative country-rock acts of the 2000s. With appearances on *Late Show with David Letterman* and *Late Night with Jimmy Fallon*, the Drive-By Truckers's already-huge fan base continues to increase.

photo courtesy of Drive-By Truckers

What's your favorite restaurant in Athens and why?

Patterson Hood: That's tough. My wife, Rebecca, and I love to do dinner and a movie at The National and Ciné. We are both film fanatics and we try to support our local art cinema all we can and the food at The National is always incredible.

What Athens celebrity, dead or alive, would you want to grab drinks with? Why?

Patterson Hood: Too many to name. One of my most treasured memories was getting to have a couple of meals with Vic Chesnutt. He was the most amazing songwriter of my generation and I was honored to become his friend towards the later part of his life. I cooked a big spaghetti dinner one night for him and Will Johnson and that evening is one I will always treasure.

If you could plan your perfect day/night out in Athens, what would you do and who would you do it with?

Patterson Hood: It would involve hanging out with my kids until their bedtime and then going out to dinner, a movie, and a rock show with my wife, Rebecca. We would end up having last call at either The Manhattan or Flicker Bar. This is such a wonderful town …

Who's your favorite celebrity chef?

Patterson Hood: Hugh Acheson is incredible. 5 & 10 is an amazing restaurant and his book is incredible.

HOLY CREPE DUO
Food Truck Owners

Kate Marsden is an Athens, Georgia, local. After college, she left and had adventures in France and around the US. She met her soon-to-be partner in both love and business, Saphir Grici, in Paris, even though he actually grew up in Bordeaux. When they met, Saphir was a scooter-riding Parisian; he never envisioned leaving until he came to Athens to meet Kate's family. He fell in love with Athens like so many people do. This couldn't have been more convenient for Kate as she is very clear on the fact that Athens is her first love.

photo by: Nicole Akstein

"For a long time I never wanted to work in business. I thought if you made a profit it had to be big corporate, no-conscious kind of work," says Kate. "Saphir really opened my eyes that owning your own business could be a service to mankind and your community." Kate and Saphir developed the idea of Holy Crepe, constantly thinking about being an enterprise with a soul. They take being good to their customers, employees, and community very seriously. They're committed to serving local fresh ingredients. "We try to take life with a good sense of humor and, by our own small works, make the world a better place."

What's your favorite restaurant in Athens and why?
Kate Marsden: My favorite restaurant in Athens is The National. I enjoy the different flavors and interesting combinations offered there. Saphir's favorite is Cali-N-Tito's. This guy reframes your flavor palate! Who can make a fish burrito one of the best dishes you've ever had in your life? Cali-N-Tito's can.

Who's your favorite celebrity chef?
Kate Marsden: The Athens celebrities we would most like to hang out with are Ken Manning and Peter Dale. Ken we've met and we're big fans of his White Tiger burgers. He also seems to share our love of fungi. Peter Dale just seems like an awesome guy, and we've been really appreciative of his support of food trucks in town.

If you could hop on a plane and go anywhere in the world for dinner, where would you go? What restaurant?
Kate Marsden: If I could magically teleport anywhere at dinnertime, it would be to our favorite neighborhood restaurant in Montmartre. Chez Toinette was the perfect hole in the wall. Two guys seemed to serve up the best food in all of Paris, while keeping the playlist hot and your wine glass full. Saphir would take us to Toto in Bologna, a pizza joint that would put most of Italy to shame. Long on handmade pizza and high-quality ingredients—short on Southern charm—this place didn't need service with a smile to keep you coming back for more.

JOSE BLANCO
Former University of Georgia Professor

photo courtesy of Jose Blanco

Jose Blanco, a Costa Rican native, moved to Athens, Georgia, in 2006 to teach in the Fashion Merchandising department at the University of Georgia. He was the associate professor in the Department of Textiles, Merchandising, and Interiors and the historic clothing and textiles collection manager. He's worked on exhibitions and given lectures at the Georgia Museum of Art, the Lyndon House Arts Center, the University of Georgia Special Collections Library, and several community organizations. He recently relocated to Chicago, but Athens still, and always will, remain close to his heart.

What Athens celebrity, dead or alive, would you want to grab drinks with? Why?

I was always a B-52's fan. I was the annoying guy who would always play their music at parties over and over. So, it would be Fred Schneider. Funny enough, I did hang out with him for a while one evening in Athens and I was having fun just talking to him. He had a baseball hat on so I did not recognize him until my friends told me later. Then, I got very nervous. I was just glad that I had not asked him a stupid question before like: "So, what do you do for a living?"

If you could plan your perfect day/night out in Athens, what would you do and who would you do it with?

Well, because I am a nerd, I would spend the morning at the Georgia Museum of Art or UGA's Special Collections Library (they have great exhibits), then have a nice lunch downtown and then walk around to see some of the downtown stores with coffee at either Jittery Joe's downtown or Big City Bread. In the evening, either a concert at the Georgia Theatre or some dancing at Little King's Shuffle Club. If I was going for a quiet night, I would then spend it at my favorite bar in town: the Manhattan Café … great cocktails and free popcorn! Certainly, I would spend my day in Athens as I have most of my days for the last fourteen years with my partner, Raúl.

Who's your favorite celebrity chef?

Oh well … I am sorry if it is too obvious but it has to be Hugh Acheson. His restaurants are as great as are his cookbooks, but I find him also intriguing as a person. I follow him on Instagram and I love the idea of someone who seems to enjoy life, the simpler things as much as the fancier ones. He has a lovely family too.

If you could hop on a plane and go anywhere in the world for dinner, where would you go? What restaurant?

Auerbachs Keller in Leipzig, Germany. I was there many years ago and I had a fantastic and memorable meal. It is not just because it is a famous place and the connection to Goethe; it was also a great meal. I would also go back to Ida Davidsen in Copenhagen in the blink of an eye; all those open sandwiches were fun and delicious.

THERESA NAPOLI
St. Joseph's Teacher of the Year & VP of Keep Athens-Clarke County Beautiful

photo courtesy of Theresa Napoli

Theresa Napoli moved to Athens in August 2003 to attend the University of Georgia. She loved the culture of the town and all it had to offer. "I knew Athens would be a great place to finish growing up!" she says. Theresa completed undergraduate and graduate school by 2010 and was lucky enough to find a job in Athens.

She currently teaches first grade at St. Joseph Catholic Parish School in Athens and serves as Vice President of Keep Athens-Clarke County Beautiful, a non-profit organization dedicated to environmental education and community outreach. They host dozens of programs each year that benefit Athens. Theresa is also a Master Composter volunteer. The Master Composter is a program offered by the University of Georgia Cooperative Extension that educates in the science and methods of all things compost. Graduates volunteer at community events all year long to educate and serve community members of all ages. To top off her busy schedule, she serves as the academic advisor for Delta Zeta Sorority. "Spending time involved with my former sorority is a nice connection to a previous chapter in my Athens life. I love to play sports as well, especially playing softball with my team, The Bruisers!"

What's your favorite restaurant in Athens and why?
This is a very hard question to answer! May I please have at least four subcategories!? If you're forcing me, I'll answer The Branded Butcher. I love the food. I love the drinks. I have literally never been disappointed with anything I've ordered there. You can tell lots of heart goes into their creations! Absolutely an experience with food.

If you could eat one dish out in Athens before you die, what would it be?
If I could eat one last meal, I'd like an appetizer of The Big Island Pizza from Ted's Most Best, followed by steak frites with whipped potatoes from Etienne, and finally a slice of white chocolate cheesecake from The Last Resort. It's my last meal, I can do whatever I want, right!?

If you could plan your perfect day/night out in Athens, what would you do and who would you do it with?
My perfect day in Athens would be with my three best friends—my soul mates—and our loves! We would start the day with a yummy breakfast/brunch at either Ideal Bagel or Ike & Jane. Next up would be walking around downtown with some delicious coffee. Next, we would head to a yoga class at Rubber Soul, then relax in the yard for a while. Utage sushi for lunch, then back home to get ready to go to Creature Comforts or Terrapin, followed by Cali-N-Tito's for dinner. We would hit the town, probably Allgood next, followed by some dancing at Little Kings, a late-night snack at The World Famous, and end the night with drinks at Normal Bar! (We like to eat and drink, what can I say!?)

If you could hop on a plane and go anywhere in the world for dinner, where would you go? What restaurant?
I would go to Japan and eat with the sushi master that David Chang did in his episode of *The Mind of a Chef!* That meal, and whole experience, seemed incredible!

THE WHIGS

This beloved Athens band has had the distinction of touring with some of the nations' most popular acts including The Killers, Franz Ferdinand, and Kings of Leon. Their frequent Athens performances have garnered them the love of the entire community with an audience that continues to grow nationwide.

photo courtesy of The Whigs

What's your favorite restaurant in Athens and why?
Parker Gispert: Taco Stand. It's a classic spot. If I haven't been in Athens in a while, it's the fix I crave most.

If you could eat one dish out in Athens before you die, what would it be?
Julian Dorio: The National's red pepper tomato bisque soup, then their lamb kefta. Peter's Middle Eastern dishes remind me of my mom's cooking (she's Lebanese) growing up.

What Athens celebrity, dead or alive, would you want to grab drinks with? Why?
Julian Dorio: I'd love to sit down with J.B. of J.B.'s Polish Sausages. The conversations I've had with him while ordering a sausage with "comeback sauce" outside the 40 Watt have always been interesting. Once he told me that, while in the army, he jumped out of helicopters with Jimi Hendrix! Could that be true?!

If you could plan your perfect day/night out in Athens, what would you do and who would you do it with?
Parker Gispert: I'd do a solo daytime walk downtown from Boulevard. Eat a Little Italy sub. Walk it off and head over to Normal Bar. Watch some Braves baseball. Head back downtown and stop at Flicker Bar, Manhattan, and The National. See a show at 40 Watt and end up at Max Canada!

Who's your favorite celebrity chef?
Julian Dorio: Hugh Acheson! It seems like everything he touches turns to gold.

If you could hop on a plane and go anywhere in the world for dinner, where would you go? What restaurant?
Julian Dorio: Ever since I saw *Jiro Dreams of Sushi*, I'm determined to eat at Sukiyabashi Jiro in Tokyo.

The State Botanical Garden of Georgia attracts thousands of visitors each year, including this Easter Tiger Swallowtail, dark morph butterfly.

WIDESPREAD PANIC

photo courtesy of Widespread Panic

Known for their amazing live shows and the frequency at which they tour, blues-inspired Southern rock band Widespread Panic has been creating a dedicated following since forming in the early '80s. Based on the strength of their musicianship, songs like the Billboard-charting "Can't Get High" and "Hope in a Hopeless World," and energetic live shows, they've managed to rank among the top-fifty grossing touring acts for eight years straight without the aid of substantial radio play, television appearances, or retail store promotion.

Dave Schools is a critically-acclaimed bass player and founding member of Widespread Panic, or "Panic" for short. He's also an accomplished producer, songwriter, and journalist with articles published in a wide variety of music magazines. Schools currently resides in Sonoma, California, with his wife and two dogs.

What's your favorite restaurant in Athens and why?
Dave Schools: I still love The Grit. It's been consistently delicious, clean, and fresh for years. Besides, I know so many of the staff (some for over 20 years) that I can just come in, sit at the counter, and catch up with old friends. Plus the desserts are outrageously evil.

If you could eat one dish out in Athens before you die, what would it be?
Dave Schools: It would be a really lengthy affair at DePalma's downtown with drinks before and then a full order of breadsticks and the classic sausage and roasted red peppers with pasta that isn't on the menu but can still be made if a chef who remembers how to make it is on staff. Hopefully, this last meal would be in the private dining room and so many of my friends would be there that the meal would never end! Think I'll stick around for a while.

If you could plan your perfect day/night out in Athens, what would you do and who would you do it with?
Dave Schools: I always enjoy showing someone from out of town around Athens, be it a relative, friend, or musician. It wouldn't really matter where we went. Who we saw around town would be more important than what we did. My experience has always been that it's the people that give a town its charm, not the places.

Who's your favorite celebrity chef?
Dave Schools: Call me crazy, but I love Gordon Ramsay. I can't vouch for his food, but I love his no-filters/no-BS attitude. Fresh and local and simple has always seemed like a no-brainer to me. Obviously superstar chefs like Hugh Acheson here in Athens, Jennifer Jasinski in Denver, and Duskie Estes where I live in Sonoma County are changing the face of dining for the better.

THE TEAM

ABOUT THE AUTHOR

Juanina Cantrell Kocher is a New York City-based food and lifestyle blogger who has worked in the restaurant industry for over fifteen years. She has worked in food PR and marketing for various chefs and is currently the events director for one of Manhattan's top restaurants. Juanina is an Athens, Georgia, local and University of Georgia graduate with a passion for all things food. This, combined with a deep-rooted love for her hometown, brought forth the idea for *Classic City Cooking*.

Visit her website at www.classiccitycooking.com and blog at www.juaninakocher.com.

photo by Ryan Kocher

ABOUT THE CONTRIBUTOR

Brittany Elyse Hodges is an Athens-based wholesale fine wine sales representative and has worked in the food and wine industry for over eight years. She works closely with restaurants and retailers in the Athens, Georgia, area, helping to build wine portfolios and promote local events that support the Athens food and beverage scene. Brittany is a University of Georgia graduate and is passionate about promoting all of the unique and creative food and beverage outlets Athens has to offer. She also manages Classic City Food & Wine's social media outlets.

photo courtesy of Brittany Hodges

ABOUT THE PHOTOGRAPHER

photo by Cora Keber

J.P. Bond is an award-winning professional photographer. Originally from La Paz, Bolivia, his family traveled extensively throughout South and Central America during his childhood. The fifteen-plus years J.P. has been working as a photographer have taken him across the world, out to sea, and even 1,400 feet underground. J.P.'s work is fresh, eye-catching, and straight to the point.

I met Juanina two years ago, and it couldn't have been better timing. When we discussed her idea, I knew immediately I wanted to be part of it, and I'm filled with pride that she chose me for this book.

In *Classic City Cooking* we made the decision to let the photos capture the essence of both the chefs' creations and the atmosphere of the restaurants serving these tasty dishes. Rather than pulling out the usual food photography styling tricks we have photographed each dish as the chefs intended them to be plated and served while showing the environment that makes each of these restaurants unique.

Through that process I feel that we have created a cookbook that is an honest reflection of the artistry put in to these dishes and is also a reflection of Athens's burgeoning food culture. I've met amazing chefs and artists in the process, but the best part is getting to taste these chefs' creations. Do I love my job? What do you think?

A huge thanks goes out to my assistants, Winston Cherry, Sarah Darradji, Greyson Ike, and Anson Trahan. They diligently keep me in check and provide immense support.

Visit his website at jpbond.com.

INDEX

5 & 10, 3, 6, 32, 59, 101

Acheson, Hugh, 3, 6, 32, 52, 101, 104, 107, 109

Agua Linda, 91

Anderson, Patrick, 76

Athens, ix, xiii; Downtown, 21, 76, 104; East Side, ix, 21; Five Points, 59, 62, 94

Automatic Pizza, 91

basil, 4, 22, 30

BBQ Sauce, 10

Bennett, Billy, 98

biscuits, 50

Blanco, Jose, 103

Blanton, Jarad, 59

Blind Pig Tavern, 91

butter, 24, 28, 45, 50, 66, 69, 72, 74, 78, 80; clarified, 22

Cali-N-Tito's, 91, 102, 104

cauliflower, 10

Cecilia Villaveces Cakes, 91

celery root, 12

chicken, 28, 62, 91, 92, 94, 95; salad, 36

Chops & Hops, 14, 17, 19

chutney, 19

Clegg, Melissa, 39

Clocked, 92

cocktails, 71, 76, 92, 95, 103; Arnold Bomber, 7; National Tonic, 56

Condor Chocolates, 92

cream cheese, 36, 78, 93

cucumbers, 56, 60

curry, 19, 30, 62, 94

Dale, Peter, 52, 71, 92, 102; foreword by, ix

Daniell, Jeff, 47

Darius Goes West, 99–100. See also Weems, Darius

DePalma's Italian Café, 21–24, 107

Drive-By Truckers, 101

Ducoté, André, 21, 24

eggs, 6, 48, 66, 74, 78; deviled, 32, 59, 94; scotch, 12; scrambled, 24

Etienne, 92, 104

Georgia Theatre, 92, 94, 98, 103

grapefruit, 43, 45, 56

grits, 43, 45, 50, 94

Heirloom Café and Fresh Market, 26–30

hoisin sauce, 60

Holy Crepe, 102

home.made, 32–36

honey, 7, 17, 80, 92

Hood, Patterson, 101

Hudson, Cooper, 47

Ideal Bagel, 93, 104

Ike & Jane, 93, 104

Independent Baking Co., 93

Iron Factory, 93

Just Pho, 93

Kelly's Jerk, 93

Kovitch, Matt, 14

La Dolce Vita, 93

lamb, 19, 62, 65, 100, 105; meatballs, 54

Lang, Mychell, 14

Lang, Patrick, 14

Last Resort Grill, 39–45, 47, 91, 98, 104

Lindsey, Gaby, 82, 84

Los Amigos, 94

Mama's Boy, 47–50

Marker 7, 94

Marsden, Kate, 102

Maumus, Mimi, 32

mayonnaise, 12, 36, 43, 60, 74

mirin, 60

miso, 60, 94

mushrooms, 34, 91; button, 34; crimini, 65

Napoli, Theresa, 104

Old Bay Seasoning, 45, 72, 74

onions, 10, 28, 54, 91, 95; green, 84; red, 4, 24, 65, 74; Vidalia, 30, 34, 36, 72; yellow, 6, 17, 19, 36, 40, 72, 86

Parrish, Scott, 59

pasta, 4, 22, 107; dough, 6; fettuccine, 22

Patel, Sachin, 59

pecans, 32, 36

Penn, Joel, 26

Phillips, Aaron, 39

pie: crawfish, 24; pie crust, 24; shepherd's, 65

pork, 19, 69, 92, 93, 94; belly, 40; shoulder, 60

Porterhouse, 62, 94, 99

Pulaski Heights BBQ, 94

Rayburn, Trey, 9

rice, 92, 93; flour, 10; green rice, 40, 42

Robert, Luke, 62

Seabear Oyster Bar, 71–74

seafood: clam, 72; crawfish pie, 24; fish tacos, 91; grouper nuggets, 94; oysters, 9, 71; shrimp, 22, 43, 45, 94; shrimp and crab cake, 74

Segars, Alicia, 47

Shokitini, 94

Smalley, Logan, 99–100

soup, 93, 94; bisque, 86, 105; chowder, 72; gazpacho, 56; squash, 30, 86

Speakeasy, 76–80

squash, 30, 94, 95; butternut, 86

Sriracha, 60

star anise, 19, 30

strawberries, 91; pickled, 30

Stubbers, Patrick, 71

Taco Stand, 94, 98, 105

The Branded Butcher, 9–12, 104

The Globe, 92, 98

The Grill, 92, 100

The Grit, 71, 93, 107

The National, ix, 52–56, 59, 71, 92, 98, 101, 102, 105

The Pine, 59–60

The Varsity, 95

The Whigs, 92, 98, 105

Viva! Argentine Cuisine, 82–86

Wallace, Andrew, 14

Wallace, Jessica, 14

Watkinsville, 14

Widespread Panic, 92, 107

World Famous, 95, 104

Zarnegar, Jamshad, 39

Spoon Me.